The TENNIS RACKET

Barry Waters

Queen Anne Press

By the same author:

Piste Again
Wish We Weren`t Here

For Andreas, Christina, Graham, John, Murphy, Norman, Twizzle
and other sparring partners

A Queen Anne Press BOOK

© Barry Waters 1984

First published in 1984 by Queen Anne Press,
a division of Macdonald & Co (Publishers) Ltd
Maxwell House, 74 Worship Street, London EC2A 2EN
A BPCC plc Company

Illustrations by Graham Thompson

British Library Cataloguing in Publication Data

Waters, Barry
    The tennis racket.
    1. Tennis——Anecdotes, facetiae, satire, etc.
    I. Title
    796.342'0207   GV996

ISBN 0 356 10593 8

Filmset by SIOS Limited, London
Reproduced, printed and bound in Great Britain by
Hazell Watson & Viney Limited,
Member of the BPCC Group, Aylesbury, Bucks

Contents

Introduction

'**KING HENRY: What treasure, uncle?**
EXETER: Tennis-balls, my liege.'

William Shakespeare, Henry V

Tennis is still optional. You don't have to play. Millions don't. But it can't have escaped your notice that the Great Game is steadily changing Life As We Know It. There are few corners of the world now where Racketeurs have not begun to take over. So much so, that it shouldn't be too long before most of the earth's surface is covered either by water or by tennis courts.

More and more people are coming to realise that you can either live your life or play tennis, and they're choosing tennis.

In Florida and California, where they do today what the rest of us do tomorrow, people live in houses attached to tennis courts, spend most of their time swotting fuzzy balls, and then as 'Super Seniors' retire to 'tennis communities', before moving on to that Great Cloud Court in the sky.

Their children have rackets put in their hands at the age of two and a youngster who doesn't have a well-developed American Twist second serve by the age of five gives serious cause for concern.

You can't walk round many suburban areas these days without hearing the echoing Pock Pock of tennis balls coming at you from some direction or other. When you're on holiday, the sound is inescapable. No one would think of building holiday hotels any more *without* tennis courts attached. If space is a problem they just put them on the roof. One of New York's newest hotels has a court on top which is open round the clock (for insomniacs who need to get up at three in the morning to hit a few) and with a professional constantly on call.

For many families, a swimming pool may still be a luxury, but a tennis court, or at least good access to one, is virtually a necessity. If a giant otherworldly air bubble goes up near your house, or something resembling an aircraft hanger, you should have no difficulty in guessing what it's for.

They are already experimenting with TV channels offering nothing but tennis 24 hours a day so that Racketeurs who are not on court can watch the super-Racketeurs slugging it out for more money than anyone in Hollywood ever got paid. Although to be fair, tennis stars are often better actors. Even the girls can now grunt like East European shotputters.

The most unlikely parts of the world are now devoting themselves to the game. Southern Spain, once famed for its bull-ranches, is now becoming better known for its tennis farms. Deeply traditional societies like Japan are having their leisure habits remoulded by tennis. The countries of Eastern Europe, which once scorned tennis as an élitist bourgeois pastime, reserve the highest honours for anyone who can beat the capitalists at their own game (and won't defect to the West). The Davis Cup has long since ceased to be a private affair between the Australians and the Americans.

Even dear old Britain, where the game used to be merely a means of enabling people to get better acquainted when the rain stopped, is catching on fast. Things have moved even faster on mainland Europe where 'le Boom' is in full swing. France, which claims to have given the world the game (including its name – from 'Tenez') is just one of the nations which has now rediscovered it with a vengeance (along with all the latest English jargon – 'un bon passing shot'); and that also goes for the Italians and the Germans and the rest. In short, it's difficult these days for any nation to hold its head up in international company, unless it has a player in the world's Top Twenty. Even the Pope is a tennis player.

Tennis used to be a seasonal affair. In England it was only around Wimbledon fortnight that people took to the parks with their warped Maxplys and last year's balls, wearing an old pair of basketball boots and with their trousers tucked into their socks. Now people are at it all year round – decked out in sunvisors and headbands, lashing out with their aerodynamically shaped rackets and grunting, for all the world, like Jimmy Connors.

The Sport of Kings, which was later taken up by wealthy English families in white flannels, long dresses and boaters who pooped balls across a sagging net on the lawn ('Anyone for Patters?') to work up an appetite for tea, has come a very long way.

It may still be called Lawn Tennis, but you are more and more likely to find yourself playing on some form of green lino. The image of a sprinkler playing gently on the grass while genteel people in whites eat cucumber sandwiches isn't quite the way it is any more. A more accurate picture would be of a group of combatants rigged out in technicolour venting their Angst on each other with the aid of some of the world's most advanced weaponry.

People don't even let up when they go on holiday. They may even take a full-time 'tennis vacation' (something of a contradiction in terms, surely). Here they continue to swot balls, often fired by a machine, or go through routines and drills, by numbers, devised by the resident tennis PhD peddling his particular 'miracle' method of coaching. All the while the victim's idiosyncracies are recorded on videotape to provide further torment after they come off court. When a particular stroke is not up to the required standard they have to slug away at it by

themselves in a 'tennis alley', probably under the stern supervision of another graduate from one of the new tennis universities.

Not every Racketeur has reached quite this level of devotion. For many there is still life after tennis. But it may not be so for very much longer. It's well known that Racketeurs who claim to lead a normal life actually spend 50 per cent of their working time on the telephone fixing up games or holding post-mortems on the previous day's match. At meetings they are always busy squeezing a squash ball in their fist to develop their wrist. On social occasions they are always on the lookout for a potential partner (someone equally ungifted). At home they no longer scold their children for breaking a window while hitting against the garage door; they simply feel guilty that they haven't built a proper tennis wall for the 'Little Lobber' to practise on.

Now it is just possible that the tennis revolution has passed you by and that you don't have a racket-stringing machine in your back bedroom. You may be one of those ordinary everyday folk who has a racket somewhere (everyone has) but have never known quite what to do with it.

If that is the case, don't despair. There is still time to join the tennis fraternity before it takes over completely. If you can't beat them, join them. You'll find you are not depriving yourself of anything. All human life is there on the tennis courts or, at least, in the completely self-sufficient world of the tennis club. Don't believe anyone who tries to tell you that tennis is only a game. You'll soon discover that it's a perfectly good alternative to life itself.

However, don't imagine it's going to be that easy. Most club Racketeurs may not appear to be doing anything very spectacular as they charge the net, gnashing their teeth, lungs bursting and blood coursing through their varicose veins. But make no mistake, it's taken them years of effort to reach that level.

This book is designed to help you to reach *your* level of incompetence that little bit quicker. It doesn't claim to be able to get you into the Tennis Hall of Fame. It doesn't even claim to be able to get you into the world's top million players. But it may just help you to survive a little better on and off the court and enable you to keep your end up amongst the ever-growing masses of the world's 'intermediate' Racketeurs.

1. Which Game?

'The human race . . . has been playing at children's games from the beginning, and will probably do it till the end'

G.K. Chesterton, The Napoleon of Notting Hill

Once you've made up your mind to become a Racketeer you've got to decide which game to play. The official game consists of hitting a fuzzy ball back and forth over a 36 inch net within a court, the winner being the person who makes the fewest mistakes.

But there are innumerable variations on this classic game played on a court against an opponent. Some people, for instance, prefer to play to an audience, while others choose to stand in the sidelines and play against other spectators. Some manage to do both – like John McEnroe who usually manages to beat both his opponents and the umpire.

It's also possible to have a perfectly satisfying match nowhere near the tennis courts: you can sit and talk tennis almost anywhere, exchanging cannonball or kicker serves for sharply angled cross-court chips or down-the-line wrist-rolling topspin backhands. Tennis is, of course, by no means the only activity where as much pleasure can be derived from talking about it as from actually doing it.

So the would-be Racketeer should decide fairly early in his career whether to have a mainly on-court role or whether to develop an off-court game (for example, as Club Official, Socialite, or Expert). In earlier days people tended to be all-rounders, at home in several tennis roles. But today the tendency, even for the average Racketeer is to specialise, and concentrate on whatever makes the best use of his natural (if modest) talents.

We will assume, however, that if you're fairly new to the game your ambitions will be to succeed on court rather than at the clubhouse bar. You probably see yourself ambling into the net behind your Big Serve, casually putting the return ball away as your opponent hurls his racket at it in desperation (and Dan Maskell intones, 'Oh, I *say* that really is the most *marvellous* volley'). Not for you the more rarefied satisfactions of scoring points in an esoteric conversation about the merits of light 16-gauge Victor Imperial gut as against a heavier string that will take a higher poundage but has less touch.

We will look at the game first, therefore, through the eyes of someone determined to make his or her mark on the clay – perhaps a park player who is tired of being accused by his friends of taking the game too seriously and is looking to move on to Better Things.

This rising Racketeer, of course, can be of either sex. Indeed in tennis, as in life, the female is often deadlier than the male. So even if, for the sake of simplicity, this

book avoids terms like Racketeuse and sticks to the masculine pronoun, it should not be assumed that it does not apply equally to the female of the species.

We will follow, then, the imaginary progress of an aspiring Racketeur as he claws his way toward his definitive niche on the club ladder. It will not be an easy journey and he should be warned at the outset that skill and virtue will not always triumph. What better illustration than that classic incident in Stephen Potter's *Gamesmanship*, when two wily veterans demolish a pair of young aces by calling into question their sportsmanship by asking them simply to: 'Kindly say clearly, please, whether the ball was in or out'.

For the game is not always what it seems. The official game often bears no relation to the deeper psychological game that may be the real purpose of the encounter. So much so that one of the first lessons a novice should learn is that it's perfectly possible to lose, abjectly even, and still win – and vice versa.

2. Getting into Gear

**'Any weekend player who doesn't use a mid-size, or
an oversized racket, is just plain nuts'**

Arthur Ashe

**'As for those oversized rackets, they're for women,
old people and cissies'**

Jimmy Connors

Equipment is a game in itself and among the first our Racketeur must learn to play. It's more complicated than it used to be.

There was a time when the only major decision you had to make was whether to wear one pair of socks or two. Everyone wore the same sort of off-white whites and played with dirty white balls and a wooden racket with an oval head (either a Dunlop Maxply or a Wilson Kramer). This was kept in a wooden press and if you were good you rubbed candlewax on the strings in the winter.

Today there is almost an infinity of choice. Rackets (or racquets if you want to be posh) are made in a bewildering variety of materials in as many different shapes – round, oval, jumbo, snowshoe, teardrop, flat-topped; some are even asymetric with tilted heads or have bent handles. These weapons of war or magic wands (depending on your style of play) are all designed to boost your ego and psyche your opponent *every* bit as much as to help you play tennis. (They are also designed to provide an income for the players who endorse them. It's no coincidence that as the number of players in the top-class game has increased so has the number of racket types on the market.) Even tennis shoes are now hi-tech, and balls also come in a number of different styles – two-toned, multi-coloured, illuminated or, would you believe, *perfumed* ('to help the concentration while serving').

Clothing is equally variegated. No longer do you just have to decide whether your motif will be a little crocodile, or a laurel wreath. Fila, Ellesse and all the rest have arrived to take up the challenge of Perry and Lacoste, and it's now impossible to buy an item of clothing or equipment that doesn't bear an advertising logo. Clothes come in full colours, pastel shades, stripes and hoops and in all manner of combinations and designs. Even conservative Wimbledon has ruled that clothing only has to be 'basically' white, allowing the *couturiers* licence for their more exotic creations – though people still tend to look as if they're playing in their underwear at '*the* Championships'.

But don't underestimate the importance of gear. Today's Racketeurs tend to have a lot; most males have more kit than Rod Laver used to tour the world with; and there are plenty of women with even more tennis dresses than Chrissie Evert.

Rules of Tennis

RAIN

When you expect it to rain, it will.

It will also rain when you don't expect it to.

The games that get rained off are the ones you were most looking forward to.

If rain stops play, it'll be when you're ahead.

If you hang around the club, waiting for the rain to stop, it won't.

If you play after it's been raining, yours will be the court with the most puddles on.

If the courts are declared unfit for play, this won't apply to the club coach.

Would-be Teddy Tinlings are always coming up with something new to pursuade them to add to their wardrobe – variations like charleston dresses, or see-through, or with rhinestones and sequins, or inverted pleats which flash a colour when the wearer moves. There are even maternity dresses for tennis-playing mothers-to-be.

Some people have a lot of gear and no game. They appear at the courts in the Spring, as soon as the nets go up, to show off their new outfits and rackets, but disappear on holiday before anyone can put them to the test.

This enthusiasm for tennis wear, even among people who don't play, means that there are now plenty of shops devoted exclusively to selling tennis gear. Or they may do tennis in the summer and skiing in the winter – a convenient combination since the clientele are basically the same people, as are the manufacturers. Even in conventional sports shops the tennis section tends to dominate the place during the summer months.

As you may have gathered from this emphasis on outward show, tennis players are no longer as modest as they once were. Much has changed since May Sutton and Hazel Wightman dared bare their elbows in the early 1900s and Bunny Austin first flashed his knees in public in 1927.

That isn't to say that even in the old days you couldn't distinguish yourself by your dress. Remember Suzanne Lenglen with her cloche hat, Jean Borotra with his beret and of course 'gorgeous' Gussy Moran with her lacy knickers. Billie Tapscott may not have been very well known when she entered for Wimbledon in 1929 but she soon was when she appeared bare-legged for her first-round match. The same with Trey Waltke in 1983, in his long cricket trousers and rolled up sleeves, looking more like something out of *The Great Gatsby* than Ivan Lendl's next opponent.

These days, arguably, there is so much variety that there's something to be said for defying fashion and sticking to the time-tested racket in the wooden press and knee-length white shorts – particularly as this carries the implication that you may not know a lot about snazzy gear but you do know something about tennis. Every club has at least one player who uses grandpa's racket and can beat just about anyone.

Rackets

But whereas it's fairly easy to ignore fashion when it comes to dress, it's more difficult where rackets are concerned. Tempting as it is to stick to the old warped Maxply (it's cheaper for one thing) most players can never quite dismiss the

suspicion that amid all the technological refinements that the manufacturers come up with there may just possibly be one that could add a little something to their game. Many a Racketeur would sell his soul for less. Those oversized jumbo rackets may not do much for your image – but can you afford *not* to play with one?

Manufacturers, therefore, vie with one another in making rackets in an ever more astonishing range of space age materials. Whether metal, fibreglass or composite, it's bound to have an impressive scientific name and will boast some special feature, or possibly several, like an enlarged sweet spot, trampoline string-ing, special vibration dampening characteristics, or more (or less) speed through the air.

Real racket freaks are into percussion centres, vibration nodes, oscillation periods, dwell times, asymetric deflections and restitution coefficients and talk knowingly about a racket with a tendency to 'torque on the volley'.

There is one particular group of racket freaks, convinced that most expensive means best, who must always have the top-priced racket on the market. Every year there's a new 'ultimate' racket for them to switch to. At this moment, somewhere in the world a racket designer is working on next year's most exclusive model. You can be sure it will have a waiting list of eager potential purchasers before it even strikes a single ball.

Shop assistants are becoming only too good at spotting likely members of this club of racket -with-the-mostest enthusiasts. And they've even begun to evolve a special technique for handling this sort of customer. It goes like this: at some point, after showing off the shop's range of standard rackets, the salesman will suddenly toss one of these lesser implements aside, will stare his victim hard between the eyes and will put on an expression designed to convey that from this customer at least the truth can no longer be concealed. Drawing closer to the client, speaking in hushed tones, and making it clear that this wonderweapon is something he does not show everybody, the salesman will then tenderly lift off a high shelf this year's most luxurious rugbeater and say:

'See this? It's too expensive of course. . . but it plays like a dream.'

If the salesman has guessed right, he need say no more. The man will be hooked.

As you might expect, the whole ritual of choosing a racket has now become infinitely more complex. Gone are the days when all you were expected to do was exchange a few words with the assistant about 'feel', swing it a few times, put it up to your ear and ping the strings and then balance its throat on your finger to check the balance. Today's Racketeur will feel he has not done himself justice if he buys a racket after anything less than half a day of intensive discussion.

Even getting it strung up is no longer a simple choice between gut and nylon. There are now almost as many types of string, in different colours, as there are rackets. People don't just talk about poundage; they specify cross-string and main string poundage. For the really demonic player there are exotic variations like diagonal stringing, bucket stringing, knotted stringing or spaghetti stringing.

But despite all this and the huge array of gear now available in most shops, the one thing you can be absolutely sure of is that you'll never be able to find exactly what you want. You'll discover that the racket you like is the one they've stopped making, or that it only comes strung in nylon, or that it is not available in your grip size or at the weight you prefer.

Thus you will usually find yourself reluctantly being persuaded by the salesman that another racket (*not* the one you came in to buy) is really the *only* racket capable of doing justice to Your Game.

The salesman will of course be quite prepared to suggest major changes to 'Your Game' if that might help you to conform to what he has in stock. Let's assume, for instance, that he has the racket you want, but only in the special long-handled version for double-handed infant prodigies. This will probably result in him persuading you (or trying to) that the only sensible solution is for you to spend the next six months or so developing a two-handed backhand.

The ritual of persuasion usually follows a fairly well-established pattern. First there will be a few sympathetic inquiries about 'Your Game'. Your replies will confirm his suspicions and his judgement as to what is the right racket for you, which he, as luck would have it, *does* have in stock. Then a few flattering parallels will be drawn between your style and the style of one of the top pros who uses this particular model. He'll then move on to the technical side which you don't understand but which tempts you with visions of the dramatic improvement you can expect with fuel-injected tension-tested malognite. To wind up there'll be the offer to knock a bit off, or chuck in the odd box of balls, finally persuading you to abandon your own better judgement.

If perchance you resist, insisting you wanted the lighter model even though *no-one but no-one*, uses it any more, the salesman may change tack and try to taunt you into buying the heavier model:

'Can't handle a couple of extra ounces, huh?'

Thus defending yourself against an experienced tennis salesman is one of the sterner tests of tennismanship, and is a skill which the aspiring Racketeur should master as early as possible.

It's a ritual that may soon extend to your having to perform on the premises. Some shops are introducing 'tennis ranges' (i.e. a wall in the backyard) so that you can test the racket out and perhaps be shamed into buying it. (How could anyone who had just demonstrated a serve as ropy as yours find the face to hold out against the expert advice of the salesman?)

Accessories

But the novice Racketeur should not be tempted to think that these choices of gear are unimportant. We all know it's how you play, not what you play with that matters and that Mac the Mouth could win your club tournament playing with a dustbin lid. But there's no need to handicap yourself unnecessarily. Your whole game could be affected by the choices you make in the shop.

A woman's service style, for instance, will be dictated by the clothes she wears. If she has no pocket in her dress (usually the case) she either has to hold two balls in her hand or leave one on the ground behind her. Alternatively she can keep the ball about her by wearing shorts or 'pockette panties' or a sort of sporran or even tucking it into her knickers. This last method was introduced to a fascinated Wimbledon crowd in 1977 by Mary Carillo, Supermac's partner in the mixed doubles. It has since rather caught on. A more modest, if less appealing solution devised by one manufacturer is a metal ball-holding frame worn at the back on a belt around the waist.

This last invention, almost Victorian in its eccentricity, is among a growing range of items for the Player Who Has Everything. There are scoring dials to clip on your racket and metal claws for picking up balls and kangaroo pouches to hold your practice balls in. Or you can have a nameplate on the butt of your racket handle or your name studded out on the shaft – in precious stones if you really want to be special.

As the number of tennis accessories has increased, so the tennis bag has become a necessity to keep them all in. It's no longer done to arrive at the court, racket in hand, with a battered box of balls under your arm in which you also keep your watch and loose change.

The manufacturers have been shrewd enough to invent rather capacious tennis bags and so encourage people to buy plenty of unneeded bits and bobs to fill them up.

Standard items in the average Racketeur's bag include various layers of warm-up clothing, towel, spare headband, wristlets, eye-shade, hat, sunglasses, sun-cream, lip-salve, assorted balls, pocket dust, resin pad, racket covers, and spare shoes, shirts, shorts and underwear.

A good deal of space will be taken up with medicaments, among them salt tablets, various types of vitamin pills, glucose, Algipan, athlete's foot powder, Ginseng, vaseline, assorted plasters, bandages, scissors, not to mention deodorants, soap, shampoo and talcum powder.

This list, of course, does not include any of the items that today's well-equipped tennis family might be expected to have at home: stringing machine, stringmeter, hypodermic and rubber glue for restoring balls, pressurised ball container, mousse balls for playing indoors, ball-marking machine, grip exercisers, indoor and outdoor ballbacks, ball firer, supply of racket strings and replacement grips, shoe goo, assortment of sneakers for different surfaces (good sliders for clay, thick bottoms for hard courts), and a refrigerator full of tennis balls. Even the washing machine will be pressed into service to launder practice balls.

The main purpose of the tennis bag, though, is to carry your rackets. As we have seen, most Racketeurs will be tempted to go through a number of racket phases – from wood to metal to composite and back again – in the course of their careers. But do remember that all the rackets displayed in your bag at any one time should be the same type. It's true that Gonzales used a more tightly strung racket for serving than he did for returning service; and that there is at least one racket on the market with an interchangeable head that can be replaced between games. But our Racketeur will probably only give himself away and cause himself much misery if he totes around an assortment of rackets and then keeps desperately swapping from one to the other between games. Failing to find the right racket is not considered to be a very good excuse.

3.Tuition

'I've had a couple of coaches and it's taken me from No. 4 to No. 40'

Diane Fromholtz

Sooner or later most Racketeurs fall into the clutches of a coach. It can happen at various stages of one's career. Some Racketeurs just can't do without their tennis guru and remain forever faithful to him. Others change coaches as fequently as they do rackets – in the hope that Somehow Someone Somewhere is going to convert their erratic backhand blockshot into the dream topspin banana curve backhand they have been seeking all their lives.

An aspiring Racketeur's first encounter with a pro often comes when he gets tired of playing with his spouse and chums in the local park. They continue to insist that 'it's only a game', whereas our Racketeur already knows that there is no life without tennis. So he decides to set out on the path to the Big Time by joining the local club, or at least *by applying to* join. No self-respecting tennis club makes joining *that* easy.

During his negotiations with the club authorities it occurs to him that there might *just* be one or two weak spots in his game that a coach *might* have something useful to say about. So he applies to sign on with one of the local pros, only to discover, in all probability, that signing on with a coach can be as complicated as joining the local club.

Coaches are invariably fully booked up – or at least they always *say* they are – and they never seem to be overeager to reorganise their diary to accommodate the self-taught *Wunderkind* from the local park. Our Racketeur may well find himself detecting a note of condescension, contempt even, as the coach looks him up and down before grudgingly agreeing to take him on – almost certainly at some inconvenient hour.

But our novice Racketeur should not be downcast. This is all just part of the usual prelude to any durable coaching relationship. The coach's aim is:

a) to establish his authority,
b) to make you feel thoroughly inadequate and much in need of coaching,
c) to bring low your confidence and performance so that when they are restored at the end of a course of lessons you will look back and say: 'What a difference. I feel so much better about my game now.'

Part of this prelude will be a preliminary hit so that the coach can size you up, and demolish any self-esteem you may have acquired. He will exchange balls with you for about five minutes, shaking his head sadly (particularly at what you imagine to be some of your better shots), and making the odd remark like, 'where on earth did you get that backhand?' His conclusion will always be that what you need is not the minor operation you requested but major surgery.

It's no use protesting that you would be driving and volleying a lot better if he took the trouble to place the ball decently for you or if he had given you the chance to warm up a bit. He'll reply that he's seen quite enough to know how you would be hitting if you were playing at your best.

At this stage, it should become clear to you which school of coaching thought your tutor belongs to. There are basically two types – the Nice and the Nasty.

The Nice Coach will even now begin to mutter a few words about certain of your shots 'having potential' and about others becoming 'natural winners' when you and he have worked on them a bit. Later in your course of lessons as you 'move up the learning curve' he'll become even more flattering. And at the end of the course your every other ball will be rewarded with a comment like, 'nice one', 'too good', 'what a get', 'all the way', 'unlucky one', 'winner', 'what a player', 'star', etc.

The Nasty Coach's remarks will probably be a succession of 'don'ts' ('*don't* slap at your shots', '*don't* roll your racket over', '*don't* push your backhand') interspersed with peremptory commands ('on your toes', 'move', 'get to it').

The Nasty Coach will be unmoved by even your best efforts. The harder you try and the better you play the nastier he gets. He tends therefore to appeal to the masochistic sort of player who believes that success is only achieved by suffering and who doesn't feel he's getting his money's worth unless he gets pushed around. You can also be sure that you'll always be the one who hits into the wind and faces the sun and does most of the fetching of the balls. You may even have to provide the balls.

At the start, though, even the Nice school of Coaches don't give you too much encouragement. They will want to spend the first couple of lessons shattering your game so that they can then rebuild it over a course of lessons, gradually bringing it back to the level it was before. Thus coaches are not normally interested in giving you just one or two lessons – they want you in thrall for a season, at the very least.

One common way for a coach to break up your game is to change a few key elements. Your grip is often one of his first targets. If you use a Western, he'll make it an Eastern; if you use a Chopper, he'll turn it into a modified Continental. It's the same with the elaborate system you have painstakingly contrived to help you serve: whatever it is, he'll dismantle it and give you another. If you like to hit the ball with slice, he'll recommend topspin. If you don't adjust your grip for backhand, he'll suggest you do. If you hit the ball on the rise, he'll tell you to hit it at the top of the bounce or as it falls. If you use wood, he'll advise changing to metal, or to whatever type he pushes. (Most coaches sell and service gear and equipment on the side at 'special' rates.)

It's no use protesting to him that all these changes are wrecking your game.

Rules of Tennis

ERRORS

You flub when you can least afford to.

The more mistakes you make, the more mistakes you make.

The more mistakes you make, the more you will talk to yourself.

Easy putaways and smashes are the shots most likely to go wrong.

The more crucial the point, the more likely you are to screw it up.

You are more likely to choke when certain people – like your coach – are walking past the court.

Your best shots will go out.

If they don't, you opponent will call them out.

You'll simply be told that re-education is always painful. It is necessary to go backwards to go forwards. In the end, though, he will assure you, your game will come good and it will all have been worthwhile.

The main thing is not to resist (or at least, not to appear to). The coach has all manner of tricks up his sleeve to bring you to heel if you do. Perhaps the most common is to confuse you by pointing out simultaneously all the things you are doing wrong. You then find yourself trying to follow instructions to correct five different things at once and get nothing right as a result. The most sensible approach is to try to ingratiate yourself with your coach and, even as he's busy squashing your ego, to help him build up his own. All coaches like to be admired and he's sure to have had aspirations as a player once (though the fact that he is coaching you probably means that these aspirations were unfulfilled). So he may well be appreciative if you put it about at the club that he once 'took a set' off one of the greats, or was first reserve for some national squad or once played Wimbledon (even if it was only in the qualifier). None of this will ever be confirmed, and your coach will probably prefer to remain a bit mysterious about it, but he certainly won't be displeased at your energetic efforts to start rumours that add to his reputation. After all, if someone as abysmal as you is capable of imagining you name and initials up on that Wimbledon centre court scoreboard, how much more real must be the dreams of this man who knows how to play a bit.

Thus showing admiration for the coach is one of the fastest ways a Racketeur can accelerate his progress. For the novice this means that the metal basketful of old balls will be abandoned that much earlier in favour of a set of six. The coach will

be prepared to move back from the net to the baseline that much sooner and you will come more quickly to the great day when he's prepared to hit with you rather than talk at you.

Some coaches, of course, are exceptions to this rule. One is the Lazy Old Boy who spends all of his time up at the net, so that he doesn't have to move too much. Most of his energy goes into offering you praise and compliments rather than into returning the ball which he does by standing at the net and blocking them back with his jumbo racket while you scurry up and down the baseline.

This sort of coach is particularly prone to break off from hitting in order to deliver a short lecture, or to demonstrate, or to scratch diagrams in the clay, or to give a tactical talk, or to offer advice about life in general. Their motto seems to be 'tell', rather than 'show and tell'. They also tend to allow a very generous slice of 'your' time to collect up the balls and tidy up the court at the beginning and the end of your encounter. You do most of the tidying up and collecting, of course.

Another coach who'll be a bit of a conversationalist is The Wise One who's espoused one of the newer methods of instruction where Eastern philosophy, or somesuch, is applied to teaching tennis, or rather *zennis*. The idea here seems to be to try to talk you into a tennis trance so that your subconscious, or rather 'Self Two' as he calls it, can do his job of showing you how to hit the ball – and save him from having to work too hard.

If you'd rather play than talk it's sometimes worth saying so, since this is by no means true of all Racketeurs. There are a growing number of pupils who come along mainly for the chat. They see the coach as a mixture of shrink, social worker and confidante – someone to tell their troubles to.

Another type worth mentioning is the Celebrity Pro. You'll know him by the price of his lessons. What you pay for, of course, is not so much his wisdom as for being able to say that you've had a lesson from the Old Maestro, or, if you are out to impress, that you once 'hit a few' with The Great Man (you won't be too specific about the circumstances, of course).

You are most likely to come across this type at a tennis 'farm', 'ranch' or 'clinic' where he will have invested some of his tournament takings. His establishment will also doubtless feature all the latest learning aids – video, ball-machines, practice alleys, 'stroke-production' machines, self-hypnosis tapes and the like. You will in fact probably spend rather more time with these than with The Great Man.

Not that these days your local coach won't offer some of these devices. There are even contraptions now for teaching you to serve – thought it seems a pity to abandon some of the traditional 'lets imagine' methods (i.e. 'lets imagine you're a pair of scissors opening,' 'lets imagine you're throwing your racket over the net').

Whatever you do, choose your coach carefully. Make sure before you start that his system suits you because you won't get him to change it. You either take it all or nothing at all. Don't imagine that because you're paying, he's there to do your bidding. He won't take kindly to being asked to just put up overheads for you and to cut out the smart remarks.

Whoever your guru is, remember that he'll always be around to plague you – in spirit, anyway. It's his criticism that will always be ringing in the back of your head and his phrases you will use when you want to curse yourself on court. And when he does appear in the flesh it'll always be at the worst possible moment. He'll invariably wander past just as you're playing a crucial point, causing you to choke as a result, bringing on a classic case of Gallway's 'Oh Oh syndrome' (as in 'Oh Oh, here comes the backhand'), and reminding you, of course, that you ought really to go back for more lessons.

4. Racketeurs

'Winning isn't everything. It's the only thing'

Vince Lombardi

One of the weaknesses of coaches is that they tend to concentrate on showing you *how* to play and not on whom to play. But though it's important to 'know the game', it's probably even more important to 'know the opposition'. The following sketches are designed to help our aspiring Racketeur to get the measure of some of his potential adversaries.

THE ADOPTER

Will probably be among the first to offer a game to the club newcomer. Is not much of a player and is probably getting on a bit. Specialises, therefore, in picking up novices whom he can 'teach' and 'advise'. It doesn't take the newcomer long to work out how to beat him but by then he'll have moved on to someone else. Takes great pride in saying that most of the best players in the club were 'brought on' by him.

THE TEENAGE PRO

Also on the lookout for innocent newcomers. This hard bitten 15-year-old semi-professional is still only a Junior member of the club and therefore needs an adult – like you – to be able to get on court during peak Senior periods. If you do 'give him a game', he'll pick the new balls out of your bag and proceed to knock hell out of them and you.

THE VETERAN

Beware. He may look harmless but this sprightly Super Senior is a wily old campaigner who knows *every* trick in the book. He'll probably encourage you to blast away at him as he piles on the points through your errors and his crafty dinks and lobs. Nothing if not humble, he will express great surprise at his victory and say: 'Well thanks ever so much. I *did* enjoy that. It's not all of you youngsters who are prepared to give an old fogey like me a game.'

THE ADVISER

Not much of a player but has an awful lot to say – about *your* game. Even if you're winning, this coach manqué will see nothing amiss in telling you to bend your knees or follow through or toss the ball up higher. This can be amusing if you're ahead, but it's insufferable if you're losing. The trouble is he's impossible to get through to. Ask him, 'Is this a game or a lesson?' and he'll probably take it as a compliment.

THE GOOD SORT

Something of an exception to the general run of Racketeurs. Usually quite talented but he wants a *friendly* game at all costs. He nees you as a pal rather than an opponent. Full of compliments, his main concern is to *see* that you enjoy the game. He won't want to beat you for fear of upsetting you. The drawback is that off-court he is a bore and once you've played him he's going to be almost impossible to avoid.

THE COMPLIMENTER

Also ever eager to praise your efforts. Will bombard you with calls of 'Shot', 'Nice one', 'Too good', and will occasionally sling his racket across court in mock desperation to pay tribute to one of your better winners. Be careful, though. Unlike the Good Sort he may just be building you up to make it easier to cut you down later on.

THE APOLOGISER

For this player, tennis means *always* having to say you're sorry. He can't stop doing it. Whether you win the point or whether he wins the point, it's the same old song. There are, however, a good many variations, ranging from the clipped 'Soi', with a mournful shake of the head, to the more cheerful singsong 'Sor-ree' (presumably when he's feeling a bit less sorry about what happened).

THE GRUNTER

He's heard McEnroe and Connors do it and he thinks it may add something to his game. There are basically two types – those who grunt *before* they hit the ball and those who grunt *after*. If before, it's usually to *your* advantage as they put most of their energy into the grunt rather than the shot. But beware of those who grunt after – it can be very offputting when you're about to return the ball.

THE MUTTERER

Mumbles to himself throughout the game, usually by way of self-exhortation: 'Come on, Harry, hit the ball. Move your feet. Step into it. Bend your knees'. Needless to say, there's very little correlation between what he tells himself to do and what he does.

THE SELF-CRITIC

Same sort of type but much harder on himself and a lot noisier: 'Move your arse.' 'I don't believe it.' 'Rubbish.' 'Come *on*.' 'Dumbo.' Often slaps his thighs to punish himself and frequently throws his racket at the fence in disgust.

COME ON ERIC! WAKE UP!

THE LOUD-HAILER

The noisiest of all. Loves bellowing out to the next court when your ball goes astray: 'Thank you, thank you, Court six.' Is always breaking off to hail passers-by: 'John. Good to see you. How's Mary? Still going on Thursday? Have one on me, won't you. Sorry, partner. Carry on. My serve?'

THE FUSSPOT

Only plays when the conditions are *absolutely* right – weather perfect, courts immaculate and the proposd twosome or foursome exactly to his liking. On court there'll always be something distracting him – like a spectator winding up his watch. He's always asking for balls to be taken again because he wasn't ready or because something moved. When it's all over he'll say something like: 'Can you ever remember a more *trying* game?'

THE EXCUSER

Spends most of his time explaining why he's not up to his usual standard (though no one has *ever* seen him at this 'usual' standard). Before the game he'll try to soften you up with tales of how his back has been playing up again or how he has the world's worst hangover. During the game he'll complain about the light, or that his racket needs restringing or that he can never concentrate when his wife is watching. If he wins, it's a miracle, *in the circumstances*. If he loses, it was to be expected.

THE FIDDLER

Always stamping and pacing, and snorting nervously. Constantly fiddling with something – adjusting his headband, straightening his racket strings, tapping the dirt out of his shoes, blowing on his fingernails. At his most irritating when he's receiving serve and you have to watch him go through his whole routine before he's ready.

THE SELF-ADMIRER

More interested in how he looks playing the shot than in where the ball goes. Probably spends a lot of time practising his strokes in front of a mirror at home. Is happiest when there are people watching, so he can take a bow if he hits a winner. His problem is that when he does happen to hit a good one he never for a moment imagines it might be returned; so he will often be caught turning to beam at the spectators as the winning ball is hit back past him.

THE REHEARSER

Brilliant at going through the motions when he doesn't have a ball to hit, but not so brilliant during a game. Whenever he flubs (often) he'll play six copybook shadow strokes just to teach himself a lesson. It's hardly surprising that as a result of all this extra activity he tends to tire early on in a match.

THE NOVICE

Doesn't know the difference between a volley and a rally or between a net-ball and a let-ball. Worse still, he's so unfamiliar with the game's *mores* that he'll ask anyone – even an established Racketeur like you – for a game. But if you do make the mistake of playing him, it won't always be as easy as you expect. His wood-shots and other unpredictable returns will win him more than a few points. And you, anxious to end it quickly, over-hit and make errors.

THE SLUGGER

Strong but not very subtle. Someone once told him what a big hitter he was so now he wallops everything he can get his racket to in the belief that he's playing The Big Game. Can be offputting at first and if even 50 per cent of his shots went in he'd be someone to fear. Fortunately, they don't.

THE RITUALIST

We all have our little ways and superstitions, but this character performs more magic rituals than the three witches. His most complex routine usually accompanies service; it often takes him many minutes to go through all his ball-bouncing, wind-ups and other little quirks. Often wins the point as a result of the sheer boredom of the receiver.

THE RETRIEVER

A difficult opponent. Often a jogger. Certainly jogs around a lot on court. He's the ultimate steady player and that's what counts in club tennis. You may think you can wear him out by moving the ball around but he can just keep pooping the ball back at you for hours on end. Eventually the errors and exasperation (yours) set in.

THE SCRAMBLER

A cruder and less successful version of the retriever. Although usually on the losing end he never gives up. Sees himself as the little guy who eats tennis shoes for breakfast and comes up swinging. In fact he's probably something of a masochist and rather enjoys taking a battering from a better player. Is sure to fall down and crash into the side netting several times in each set as he lunges for ungettable balls.

THE GROUNDSMAN

Always seems more interested in preparing the court than playing the game. Will invariably waste time before you start watering or rolling or sweeping the court. Then he'll have to check the net and clean the lines and clear away various bits of grit. Sets the court up so nicely that it's a pity to spoil it by playing on it.

THE BRAIN

Can't play very well but is convinced he has a fine Tennis Mind. When his shot sails hopelessly out he'll explain that if it had gone where he wanted it to go, it would have been a sure-fire winner: 'You see I drew you forward and created the space, but I just couldn't place the ball properly with my down-the-line backhand drive'. Is usually happier at the bar than on court.

THE TANTRUM-THROWER

Watches tournaments on television and feels it's the done thing to blow up from time to time. Enjoys his reputation as the club Nastase and rather imagines that people also say of him: 'He may be temperamental, but my God he's got talent.' They don't and he hasn't.

THE ONCE-A-YEARER

Gets the urge for a few days every year, usually when inspired by some big tournament. In Britain it's usually Wimbledon that brings him down to the club in his new outfit convinced that this is going to be *his* year. Soon discovers what he discovers every year – that it ain't that easy. Retires after a week or so to nurse his blisters and resume his career as an armchair player.

THE SAINT

Always gives you the benefit of the doubt. Calls his own serves out and is the first to insist that his shot was long. Frequently makes mistakes with the score in your favour. Either he's a very good player and can afford the points, or he wants something in exchange (like your spouse), or he's a very subtle gamesman. He may, of course, be just plain stupid.

Rules of Tennis

WINNING AND LOSING

Losing makes winning worth while.

He who makes the fewest mistakes, wins.

He who hits the most winners, often loses.

You are more likely to start talking to your opponent when you're winning.

When you're losing, you are more likely to start talking to yourself.

When you win, it's usually on a back court with no one watching.

When you lose, it's usually in full public view.

If you try to change a losing game, you will lose by even more.

The more you lose, the more you are likely to lose.

Losing is more tiring than winning.

Your tennis elbow or your bad back are more likely to come on when you're losing.

Most losses are blamed on the court, the racket, or the weather.

Most wins are credited to your playing skill.

THE JOKER

Usually more of a doubles player. Full of remarks like: 'Right shot, wrong court'. 'Ace coming up.' 'What's it to be – cannonball or twister?' (He can do neither.) 'Well you put that one away. I'm going to have to stop giving you these easy balls.' Also specialises in what he imagines to be trick shots – like *trying* to hit the ball between his legs.

THE CHOKER

Basically a good player, but goes to pieces on key points. Obsessed with the score, you can almost hear him thinking to himself: 'Well, if I lose the point it's 4 – 3 to him, then it's his serve, then I'm serving into the sun, and by that time Freda will be along, and before you know it she'll have told Mary that I lost to Tom'.

THE UNFORTUNATE

Most Racketeers fall into this category quite frequently. It doesn't take much to make us feel that the tennis gods are against us, that our opponent wins all the netcords, that we get all the bad bounces and spend our time chasing fluky woodshots. Each misfortune will be accompanied by an appropriate expression of despair: 'I just don't believe it.' 'How many more times.' 'Am I unlucky or am I unlucky?'

THE RACKET CHANGER

Another relative. Knows more about rackets (of which he has many) than he does about tennis. Is always swapping them between games or making adjustments. Goes through a number of different racket types in the course of a season. (He's worth knowing if you're looking for a virtually new racket at a knock-down price.) Firmly believes that one day he'll find the magic racket that will do his playing for him.

THE BUREAUCRAT

At his busiest when changing ends. Records game scores on a special scorecard and then makes notes about how he's doing. Has total recall for points played. If he's not playing well he fishes out one of his checklists to try to find out what's going wrong. In the next game you'll see him trying to play strokes by numbers.

THE BALL-COLLECTOR

Has a tennis bag full of balls – some in cans or boxes, some loose, all different colours. Is always adding to his collection and usually manages to leave the courts with more balls than he had when he started. Is also rather deft at exchanging his dud ones for other people's new ones. After the game he first rushes off to find all the balls and then remembers to shake hands – if his opponent is still around.

THE BALL MISER

A cousin. Has an unopened can or box of tennis balls in his bag and his aim is to see that they stay unopened all season. Always offers his balls that little bit too late or puts you off with a remark like: 'I don't know if we want to open a new box just for a half-hour knock'. If he is forced to use his balls (which will be heavily marked to show they're *his*) the game will be constantly interrupted by his shouts of: 'Have we got all the balls?' Everyone is then dispatched to search for the missing ones while he conducts ball-checking negotiations with the neighbouring courts.

LADY WITH FRILLY KNICKERS

Several at every club. Usually buxom and middle-aged. Convinced that her fancily decorated derrière under shortish skirt is one of the main attractions on court. She's often right. Both sexes tend to take an interest. The bonus for her is that no one takes much notice of her tennis.

THE PRACTISER

Doesn't play, just practices – usually against the wall. He will occasionally agree to a hit but will never be lured into a game. Usually makes some excuse, like he'd rather not risk a match till he's ironed out some kink in his backhand.

THE NIGHT-OWL

Often a youngster or a wall-basher or some other keen practiser. Refuses to accept that the days are getting shorter and will continue to bang balls at the wall or at another night-owl till well past dusk. Presumably they *hear* where the ball lands – they certainly can't see it.

THE INTERRUPTER

Often found in pairs. They walk behind your court or cross it during a point. They hit balls onto your court and then ask for them back while you're still playing. If you don't get their ball immediately they invade your court during your game, hardly even bothering to duck, and get it themselves. If you get nasty, they get upset and make you feel like the offending party. Sometimes of course they are pretty young things, in which case male players just smile and say 'Any time'.

THE YEAR-ROUNDER

Prefers to play in winter, rather than summer – perhaps because there's less opposition then. He usually manages to find the odd person to play with – either someone who can't wait to try out the new racket he got for Christmas or someone trying to get fit again after a rugby injury. When the tennis season arrives he just fades away or claims he's injured. He'll be back on court around New Year's Day, swinging away in sub-zero temperatures, clad in furlined tracksuit with a couple of scarves around his neck, racket-handle emerging from his special mail-order 'winter tennis' mittens.

5. Games Racketeurs Play

'Serious sport has nothing to do with fair play'

George Orwell, The Sporting Spirit

Now that our novice Racketeur can recognise the enemy, he must become wise in ways to play him. One of the most important things he must decide is whether he wants to win fair and square or whether he wants to win at any price. If the former, then either you're not telling the truth, or you're too good a sportsman to be a real Racketeur. At all events, this chapter is not for you.

Don't misunderstand. The average Racketeur is usually a decent enough sort. He's definitely not the sort of person who puts Vaseline on his opponent's racket handle before the game. On the other hand he may not quite be able to put his hand on his heart and swear that he always admits it when an opponent's ball ticks the edge of his racket before sailing out of court. In short, he's a little bit less of a decent sort when he's swinging a tennis racket.

Put it another way. Experience has taught him that there's no such thing as a *friendly* game of tennis, and that, nice fellow though your opponent may be, he wants nothing less than to leave the court spattered with your blood. He knows that when you're on court, the world is against you. There will be bad calls, bad bounces and people irritating you on the sidelines or in the next court. The bad breaks just won't even themselves out. It's always your opponent's net balls that will have legs and climb over to drop on your side of the court.

It's only natural, therefore, that the Racketeur should try to level things up a bit. One way to do this is by mastering as many as possible of the other games that go on before during and after a tennis match. For tennis, as we have seen, is not one game but many. Here is a rundown of some of the other games that Racketeurs play.

The Pre-Game

'Many matches are won in the changing room beforehand'
Yannick Noah

The outcome of many matches is decided before the game even starts. It's all a question of knowing how to play either of the two roles that can fall to you – that of Superior Player or that of Challenger.

If you're the Superior Player, make sure your opponent knows it. Turn up late and when you arrive, take your time. Leave him to roll and water the court and sweep the lines. Ask him to crank while you (the Precision Player) check the height

of the net. If you can manage a few press-ups while he is busy with his court chores, so much the better. If you have better equipment, flaunt it to show that even in this department, he is at a disadvantage. Condescend, after inspecting them carefully, to use his balls. Make him walk to the far end when you start to play. (He has no choice but to accept this treatment because he's supposed to be grateful for the game.)

If, instead, you are the Challenger (and there may be a certain conflict of opinion over who is to play which role) your best course is to be excessively humble and sycophantic. ('Don't know if I can give you much of a game.')

You can, in fact, be much better off as the underdog. The more you build your opponent up as you inspect and admire his £300 racket, the more he will have to live up to it and the more pressure he will be under. If you also let him detect a note of irony in your admiration, it could sow the seed of doubt in his mind that will later lead to his downfall.

A certain amount of ambiguity in your remarks can also pay dividends in undermining his confidence. Try:

'I suppose with your sort of game it pays to have a racket like that'. (Could mean that he needs a super racket to boost his lousy game or that only a super racket can do justice to his game.) Or:

'You've been taking lessons, haven't you?' (Could mean that he needs them or that he looks in good shape.)

Rules of Tennis

BALLS

The big question before the game is: 'Whose balls?'

The first question afterwards is: 'Do we have all the balls?'

If there is a hole anywhere in the side netting, the ball will find a way through it.

There is usually at least one ball missing.

There is *always* a ball missing if they are
a) new
b) yours.

New balls get lost faster.

The more energy you put into looking for a ball, the less likely you are to find it.

The person who puts the most energy into looking for a ball is its owner.

If it's your ball, people will stop looking that much sooner.

The people on the next court will invariably be playing with the same type of ball as you.

Theirs won't be marked either.

One of the most difficult decisions in tennis is whether to buy a set of four or a set of six.

Whatever happened to white tennis balls?

The Knock-Up

'When we have match'd our rackets to these balls,
We will in France, by God's grace, play a set'

William Shakespeare, Henry V

Here, also, there are two basic approaches. You can either overwhelm and demoralise your opponent by a display of sheer class – if you're up to it, that is. Or you can turn the knock into a bit of a shambles, giving no hint of your better shots and sneaky point-winning ways.

If your aim is to overwhelm, proceed as follows. Ignore any balls that are not hit right to you, looking vexed if more than a few go wide. Get to the net first and stay there, making him stretch for your putaway volleys and generally establishing a master-pupil relationship. Look very annoyed if he has the impudence to try to pass you. Assume that he is there to service you. If he looks as if he wants to come to the net, give him another job to do, like putting up overheads for you ('A couple of lobs please').

When you're back at the baseline, keep asking him for a particular placement, like hitting to your backhand. He'll then have to concentrate so hard on providing what you want that he'll forget to practise what he wants.

Do everything with as much style as you can muster. It doesn't matter in the knock-up if the ball goes in or out, so you can afford to stay loose and hit with a bit of a dash even if you can't keep the ball on the court. If *he* starts hitting long, of course, that's a different matter and he should be made aware of your displeasure. Don't peel off any clothing during the knock. In fact, if you can manage it you should try to keep your tracksuit on for the duration of the game itself.

The shambolic approach to knocking up is perhaps more fun and probably easier since most Racketeers have more talent for bad tennis than good. Your aim here is to give him as little practice as possible, to spoil his game and to lull him into a false sense of security with your abject play. Hit long and wide and try to beat him, so that he hardly ever gets a racket to the ball. When he comes to the net, pass him with every other shot, all the time mumbling: 'Sorry. Can't seem to keep hold of it today. This really is terrible. I'm not usually this bad.' He may even react sportingly and keep setting the ball up nicely for you just to try to bring you back to your normal game. You, of course, give no clues as to what that normal sneaky game really is. You spring that on him when you start to play.

But however satisfying it is to get your way in the knock-up, remember that its main purpose is to set you up for the game that follows. It's not much use winning the knock-up, if you then proceed to lose the match.

Off-Court Play

**'Some games offer more opportunities than others
for life-long careers and are more likely to involve
relatively innocent bystanders'**

Dr Eric Berne, Games People Play

The aim here is to convey that the game with your opponent is only a minor matter and just one of a number of things your are currently involved in. Thus, you are always interrupting the game to make or take telephone calls (this needs to be arranged in advance), or to move your car, or to fetch your watch which you forgot in the changing-room.

You will also keep stopping to chat to people watching or to exchange remarks with the players on adjacent courts or to halt a passer-by to ask about the latest score in the Davis Cup match.

By creating a rapport with spectators through this almost constant dialogue you make your opponent feel he's not playing you but also the people on the sidelines. Even if they are ribbing you about *your* game your opponent is likely to feel they're on *your* side rather than his. If *he* has any friends or supporters watching be sure to make contact with them too; and when he hits a winner make some patronising remark to them, like 'He's too good for this game, isn't he?'

Once you've set things up with the spectators, make use of them. Put up a few lobs or any other shots that are much more difficult to play if there are people watching. He's sure to flub them. There are few things more demoralising than playing against a part-time opponent who doesn't seem to care if he wins or loses, and against half a dozen spectators.

The Talk Game

'Please tell me what I said'

John McEnroe to Wimbledon umpire in 1983

Whereas in off-court play you spend most of your time talking to the spectators, here you spend most of the match nattering away to your opponent.

This is a game that should really only be played against someone who doesn't want to talk – the introverts, or people who thrive on private pent-up aggro, or who need quiet to concentrate or who simply prefer to have a tennis relationship with you, and not a talking relationship.

It's very important to pick the right kind of talk, i.e. the sort best calculated to annoy and upset your opponent. It may be mumbling and swearing at yourself, or

giving your opponent some patronising advice, or lavishing praise or sympathy upon him, or just making chirpy comments to pass the time of day, about the weather or the state of the nation.

The key to it all is timing – chiming in with yet another of your friendly observations at exactly the right moments, i.e. when your opponent is at his most brittle.

But talking is not always the right thing to do. Some people relax and play better when their opponent chatters away at them. It makes them feel the match is more of a social event than a competition. With these types, it's silence and frozen glances that will win the day.

The Injury Game

> **'After the year of the thumb (Bjorn Borg, 1978), the year of the groin (too many to name, 1979), the year of the shoulder (Pam Shriver, 1980), and the year of the back (Tracy Austin and others, 1981), we arrived at the year of the previously unheard of. . . Martina Navratilova caught toxoplasmosis'**
>
> *Ian Barnes*, The Tennis Times

Most Racketeers play this game – they all suffer from backache, torn ligs, tennis elbow or something – but they play it in different ways.

First, there are the Walking Wounded. These are tennis warriors, proud of their calloused hands and taped-up fingers, who wear the scars of battle almost as part of their tennis outfit. The head bandage or strapping on arm or thigh are there mainly for effect, gamely worn, with a hint of rakishness. They see themselves as tennis musketeers, bravely carrying on regardless, the bandages all part of the image.

Next, there are the Talking Wounded – perhaps the most common type, who use their injuries as their main excuse. From the moment they meet their opponent to the moment they step on court, most of their talk will be of the woes and ailments from which they are currently suffering. The aim is two-fold: to soften up their opponent (fat chance) and to give themselves a let-out if they lose or play badly.

So common is this approach that you will frequently find two opponents energetically exchanging details of their ailments and agonies and, in effect, competing with one another to be the least likely to survive the match.

Some players continue to parade their injuries during the game – a well rehearsed limp, gritting their teeth in pain from their tennis elbow, or intermittently clutching the part of their body they claim is giving them trouble. Provided they get the sympathy they feel they deserve, they usually offer a stiff-upper-lipped: 'Don't mind me. Let's play on'. But they can sometimes use their disabilities as an excuse to pull out of the game if they don't like the way things are going.

A variation of this game is to take your time before revealing your disability. You say nothing about it before the match and give no sign of suffering when you start to play. It's only at some crucial moment when you need to turn the game around that you stoically bite your lip and reveal ('No. No, it's nothing, really') that you only have a few days to live.

The Change-Ends Game

**'When they change ends they take the whole minute and
a half because nobody wants to be the first to get up'**

Vic Seixas

Like other off-court games, this can be as hard fought as the match itself. Normally the ordinary club 'friendly' doesn't allow for the full Wimbledon ritual of sitting and towelling and barley water drinking (or brandy-swigging, in the case of Suzanne Lenglen). But despite the pressure on court time, today's Racketeurs are making more and more of the change-ends break, not just to take a breather, but also to grapple with their opponent at close quarters.

Some types of players find it particularly useful – notably those who go in for off-court play (plenty of scope for contact with spectators) and those who have perfected their own special change-ends ritual (like McEnroe tying and untying his shoelaces and Connors reading his letters). This can make it rather frustrating for those who haven't developed much of a change-ends game and just stand there wiping their racket handle on the net cable.

Even the simple process of passing your opponent, without any hanging about on the bench, is an art in itself, offering great opportunities to the masters of eye contact.

This is when an apparently casual remark about your opponent's 'cracking forehands' or his 'lethal underspin offensive lob' can change the course of a match. Praise for your opponent's best shot – the one that has been doing all the damage to you is a sure way of guaranteeing that this shot will from now on start to fall apart. This is because once you've paid tribute to his forehand or his lob he will be conscious of it, start thinking about it, and try to hit it that bit harder. Therein lies disaster. Even a fairly general remark like, 'You're playing well' can have a more devastating effect on your opponent's game than all the artillery you can muster.

Scoring

**'Learn all the rules, every one of them, so that you
will know how to break them'**

Irvin Cobb

Most Racketeurs are more interested in finishing the game with a good score than in having played a good game. After all, if they score well, they can easily delude themselves that they played well.

At all the events, for the average Racketeur results count. The best way to see that they count in your favour is to take charge of the bureaucracy of the game right away. Make sure you spin the racket for service. There's no need, incidentally, to leave it lying around long enough to enable your opponent to see if it really was rough or smooth. Many people don't know the difference, anyway.

The bizarre scoring system used in tennis is of course to your advantage – especially against a stronger opponent. You may go down 6 – 0 in the first set but then manage to hang on desperately to salvage the second by the skin of your teeth. You thus walk off the court with one set each, even though by any objective test you are the loser. (A deciding set is not recommended in these circumstances.)

If you keep the score it also enables you to orchestrate the game in your favour. For instance, in a match such as the one just described, you can afford to be very generous to your opponent in the *first* set. He'll be so far ahead anyway that there's nothing to be gained by cheating him of the odd point. Give him the benefit of all the doubts (making sure, of course, that he knows it). At all events you can never do much about a player who's on a hot streak. It's best to just battle on and wait for his game to go off. It always does sooner or later.

It's in the second set that you recoup for your generosity in the first. As you struggle to stay in the game you claim back everything you gave away in the first, with interest, plus anything else you can get away with.

The point is that there's nothing absolute about scoring. It's more in the nature of a bargaining process. You give a little here to gain a little there. And if *you* do the scoring you can make sure you gain at the right times. It also gives you a definite psychological advantage, if the other player is always asking you what the score is. Being scorer also means you can upset your opponent at crucial moments by calling the *wrong* score. But make sure when you do this that you've got your version of events clear in your mind so you can rattle off: 'The first ball went wide, remember, and then you double-faulted and then it must have gone to 15 – 30 because we were in the ad. courts. . .'.

And don't overlook the possibility of calling the score wrong in *his* favour. We all like something for nothing and this can have the effect of disarming him and making him believe the gods are with him at a time when you're trying to lower his defences. There's no point in being a consistent meanie – especially over unimportant points. And it leaves you free to claim the important points.

The Delaying Game

'Play up! Play up! and play the game!'

Henry Newbolt, Vitae Lampada

The rules say that play shall be continuous. But it will often be in the Racketeer's interest to see that it is not. The delaying game is useful in all kinds of circumstances. You may want to break up your opponent's rhythm if he's on a hot streak, or you may simply need a breather. Here are a few ways you can control the pace of the game:
– Get cramp
– Get something in your eye

- 'Lose' your contact lens
- Tie your shoelace, blow your nose, wipe your glasses, towel off the sweat
- Remove an item of clothing (wear plenty so you can do this at regular intervals)
- Be distracted by people and events off court
- Cause confusion about the score ('Didn't I win the second set?')
- Find an excuse to leave the court (telephone call, move car)
- Court maintenance (filling holes, removing grit, cleaning lines, adjusting net)
- Call for ball inspection ('Isn't one of those balls dead?' or 'Have we got all the balls?')
- Take time regrouping balls (clearing balls off court, returning balls to adjacent courts, gathering balls for service)
- Hit a ball out of court and into the nettles (especially if they are *his* new ones)
- Make opponent repeat serve (distraction off-court, alien person or ball passing by, or you weren't ready, or 'Didn't that ball brush the top of the net?')
- Use your slowest service wind-up (with much ball bouncing).

The After-Game

'Say nowt, win it, then talk your head off'

Brian Clough

Once you've said 'Thanks for the game' and collected the balls, things are by no means over. There will then be a post-mortem, usually at the bar, when you decide whether you *both* enjoyed the game and want to play again, whether only *one* of you enjoyed the game and wants to play again, whether *neither* of you enjoyed the game and there will on no account be another game.

This after-game, which is basically an attempt to square two different versions of what happened, can be as fiercely contested as the real game – especially by the loser. As often as not, he will feel that he didn't *really* lose, or that he wouldn't have lost if circumstances had been a bit different and if fate had not conspired against him. His tributes to the winner will be along the lines of 'you really were on today,' implying that it was only because he was, somewhat exceptionally, 'on' that he won.

Even someone who goes down 6 – 0   6 – 0 is perfectly capable of portraying this as a close encounter – particularly to third parties. To the question 'how did you get on?' he might respond, somewhat ambiguously:

'The ball wasn't exactly rolling for me, I'm afraid.'

'It went his way in the end – but I think we both enjoyed it.'

While the loser tries to minimise the margin of his defeat, the victor will usually seek to widen the gap – particularly if things really were close and he only won by a couple of fluky netcords in the tiebreaker in the fifth set.

He'll want to make sure he exacts the proper deference from his victim and is not deprived of the privilege of explaining to him what he did wrong and how he could improve his game. (The price of defeat is often a lecture from an equally incompetent player.)

A winner who has a more comfortable margin of victory can afford to be more gracious. After all, he may want another ego-boosting game with his opponent sometime.

'I don't know how I win – in some ways you really play much better tennis.'

'It was one of those days when everything seemed to be going for me.'

This sort of consolation comment is very important to many regular losers. And to earn these tributes they are often prepared to do an awful lot of grovelling, with remarks like: 'I'm afraid I'm not really in your class'. The victor then replies with another pat on the back:

'Nonsense – it could have gone either way.'

'Don't be so modest – it was touch and go a lot of the time.'

But some losers just won't accept defeat. They will always find some reason or other to suggest that it was not a proper game: they were working on their backhand; or they were trying out a new racket; or they thought it was 'just a hit'.

And that's when they are in the company of their opponent. When it comes to explaining events to others they'll permit themselves even more artistic licence. It's one of the curious things about tennis that there are plenty of players and plenty of winners, but very few real losers.

6. Serving

'The best way to die would be serving an ace at Wimbledon'

Jean Borotra

For many Racketeurs the Moment of Truth comes when it's their turn to serve. Unfortunately none of the strategies we've mentioned so far can do much to help you through this ordeal.

Those early Real Tennis players, the kings of medieval times, didn't much enjoy serving. Feeling it was beneath their dignity, they used to get a servant to put the ball into play for them – hence the term 'service'. For today's Racketeur, however, there is no such way of avoiding this chore.

Serving is probably the most difficult thing you have to do in tennis. It should be the easiest. After all, you've just got to hit the ball over the net, in your own time, while nothing else is going on. It's the same shot every time and, in theory, gives you a distinct advantage.

Rules of Tennis

YOUR GAME

If you think your game can't get any worse, you're wrong.

All Racketeurs are invariably 'off their game'.

Whenever you think you've found your game, it will disappear.

The day you're on top form is the day you lose.

The harder you try, the worse you play.

Your best shots will always surprise you more than your worst shots.

The stroke you've been practising is the one that won't work.

A sure way to wreck your game is to watch a big match and then go to the club and try to play like the people you've just been watching.

Whatever you're doing wrong, someone will tell you to bend your knees more.

Games that start well, often don't end well. The converse is not true.

All Racketeurs believe that there's a day when it will all come right.

It won't.

And yet most Racketeurs can't do it – at all events, not very well. They can do it in their mind's eye; they can do it without the ball. But out there on court with people watching and their opponent hopping about to distract them and showing his contempt by standing a yard inside the baseline, their speed-of-light in-swingers never seem quite to come up to expectations.

There are as many service styles as there are players, most of them better left undescribed. Indeed, if tennis is a uniquely revealing sport, the most revealing single moment is when a player places his foot parallel to the baseline, teeth gritted, psyche bared, and attempst to put the ball into play.

The range of mannerisms, twitches and other assorted idiosyncracies is almost infinite. No two serves resemble one another, except in the end-result – the patsies or marshmallows or net-balls or way-outs that come off the racket.

In theory, serving should be when you dominate. If you never lose your serve, they say, you can never lose the match. But really it's only the pros who usually make games go with serve. At club level, it very often doesn't matter who serves. It may even be a disadvantage: you parade your weakness and tire yourself out.

Most Racketeurs are rather ashamed of their serve. But some put a brave face on the whole business and try to mask their technical shortcomings by sheer power and much whirring of arms. They see themselves as a 'coiled spring' delivering the sort of 130 mph cannonball that Roscoe Tanner, Steve 'The Bull' Denton or Big

Chip Hooper would be proud of. (It is, incidentally, one of the great mysteries of tennis how certain famous serves can be judged to travel at *exactly* 147 mph, or whatever).

Other Racketeers try to lie low on service, getting it over as quickly and unobtrusively as possible. No elaborate wind up, they just poop the ball over the net with a short half-swing as if they were playing badminton, trying to get the ball into play without anyone noticing.

Most players, however, make more of a meal of it, going through all manner of elaborate mumbo jumbo and ritual as they position themselves, bounce the ball, wind up and launch into their complex gyrations.

Some of these serves clearly owe their eccentricity to the performers' belief that one particular part of the serve is the key to it all. It may be backflex, or backscratching with racket or a high toss or wrist flicking. Whatever it is, this feature will be exaggerated out of all proportion to the rest of the action and will be the main reason why the whole service is out of sync.

Not that the server will be aware of this. Very few people have any idea what their serve actually looks like. This gap between perception and performance makes for some profound shocks when people see themselves on video. Some people never recover.

But though we may not be able to see ourselves, we are only too good at observing other people, and giving them the benefit of our observations. Serving is yet another aspect of the game where everyone has some advice for everyone else – about tossing the ball, or 'throwing' the racket, or ending up with belly-button facing the net-post.

No serve, of course, stays the same. While the pros vary their twists and their spins and their placements, your serve will vary itself of its own accord. Not only do no two people serve alike, no two serves from any one Racketeer are ever the same.

The one thing you can be sure about is that if, amazingly, your serve seems to be working, it will, after a while, go off (sooner rather than later). Your service will come and go throughout your career. You'll never reach a stage when you finally get the hang of it. But you'd better keep trying – because until they decide on a machine to put the ball into play, you're going to have to keep on performing this humiliating task yourself.

7. Calling

'Pietrangeli. . . has invented a new method of helping linesmen make favourable decisions on close calls. This consists of placing a ball on the spot where he would like the linesman to believe the ball has bounced. Here in Rome, where he is regarded at least as a God, the method invariably works to perfection'

Gordon Forbes, A Handful of Summers

Whereas serving is something you may never be able to do properly, calling is an art that no self-respecting Racketeur can afford not to master.

In theory, it's very simple: you call your side; he calls his side; if you're not sure whether it's in or out you play it as good.

Well that's the theory, reflecting perhaps the origins of the game as a pastime for gentlefolk who could be expected to *do the right thing* and resist those temptations to call a good ball out.

But today, as we know, the Racketeurs have taken over, and their attitude to calling is much more pragmatic. The theory may not have changed, but practices have.

The Racketeur knows that you can't win just by hitting good shots – you have to get them *called* in as well. He knows that however much we may *think* our ball into the corner or *hope* our opponent's ball out, it doesn't always land where it should. Practical measures are needed to see that the point is recorded in our favour, which basically means *calling out as many of your opponent's balls as you can get away with*.

That isn't to say that there is no place for the more old-fashioned approach. As Harold Macmillan once said: 'There are times when the right thing to do is the right thing to do'. So it always helps if you do manage to come over as the sort of person for whom tennis was originally designed – that is to say, a decent well-bred type whose honour should not be lightly impugned.

A Racketeur who really succeeds at conveying this impression won't even need to stoop to querying a bad call by his opponent – not out loud anyway. All he need do is hesitate for a moment, looking rather hurt and surprised, and just possibly raising his eyebrows. This performance of 'a gentleperson wronged' should be enough to shame his opponent into calling the next five doubtful balls good.

Sometimes the Genteel Racketeur can even get an opponent to reverse his original call just by shooting him a glance that is the equivalent of the Wimbledon umpire's 'Did you call, linesman?' thus giving him the chance to change his mind.

Even if you don't manage to pose as a Genteel Racketeur a little consideration for your opponent's feelings can go a long way. Apologise handsomely when you have to disallow his ball, or indeed for any of your dirty tricks such as lobbing into the sun, or into the lights when you play indoors, particularly in the early stages of a match:

'Sorry – and such a good shot, too.'

'Just a little long, I'm afraid.'

'So good – but just out.'

'You *are* having such bad luck today.'

'You couldn't have got any closer and still missed.'

It makes you opponent feel a lot better if you congratulate him on his shot before telling him it was out. Appear disappointed rather than gleeful, when his ball is long. Your aim is to appeal to his better nature: if he calls a doubtful ball of yours in, say 'thank you' – it may tempt him to do it again.

To really start earning his good will, though, you have to call *some* of his balls in – making clear by your tone, of course, that there was considerable doubt as to whether these balls were *really* in. The extent of your generosity will depend a bit on how the game is going. As we observed earlier with regard to scoring, it's when you are comfortably ahead or comfortably behind that you can afford to give points away, putting your opponent in your debt for when you need the points later on.

Don't think an opponent will appreciate your charity points any less when he's being well beaten. We've all experienced that sense of panic when our opponent goes three games up at the start of a set and we wonder, in some desperation, whether we are going to get any games at all. No one likes to lose 6 – 0.

Gentility and generosity, however, will take you only so far – particularly if your opponent is playing the same sort of game. You may both start out by trying to outdo one another in your display of magnanimity and virtue. But sooner or later, you can be sure, things will degenerate.

We'll then see the more familiar side of the calling game. No more dignified silences and turning the other cheek. 'Are you sure it was out?' We will splutter marching over to the opposite side of the net to point aggressively at the spot where it is alleged that the ball landed. Usually, on such occasions, there is nothing to indicate that the supposed mark was, in fact, made by the ball in question. But this action of pointing at the spot is held to have a curious authority. Even when playing on some unmarkable surfaces like concrete or lino, players will solemnly walk over and point to a spot where a ball travelling at 70 mph is held to have been in contact with the edge of a white line for four milliseconds.

At this stage of the game, it's bare-faced gall that counts. If you're going to cheat, cheat confidently. No late calls when you've mulled over the situation. *Call it out straightaway*.

By now, you'll be using the more standard euphemisms for 'out' – like 'sorry', 'away', 'nooo', 'long', 'just wide', 'double', 'fault', etc. You may even simply say 'out'. (Never, incidentally, say *definitely* out as this implies you may not be sure.) At times, to lend specious authority to your bogus claims, you may resort to the most bare-faced exaggeration: 'A yard out' or 'a racket's length away' you pronounce, holding up your hands as if demonstrating the size of the fish that got away.

No raised eyebrows now when your opponent calls your ace serve out. 'What do you mean, out?' you will protest. Or, if you prefer the ironic approach: 'Was that a bit fast for you to see then?' If your opponent sticks to his guns, don't let the matter rest there. 'OK', you should mutter bitterly, 'if you really need the point that much.'

The out-calls will now come thick and fast and although it's generally best to deliver them straightaway, with assurance, and without hesitation, there are occasions when it's best to hold your tongue.

For instance, when you are playing an opponent who likes to rush in behind a big serve, it pays to delay your call until he's well into his charge. *It's a good way of*

wearing him out. Alternatively, don't say anything. Just wait a second or two and then prepare to receive serve again, *in the same service box.*

Not calling is also a good way of keeping a point in reserve if you should need it later on. Even if your opponent is wise to how a doubtful uncalled ball can subsequently be used against him, he'll probably resist the temptation to ask you to call it; if he does, it simply confirms that he has doubts about the ball, leaving you to call it out there and then. He is more likely, in fact, to wait a while and then innocently ask what the score is (by which time you may be in a better position to know if you need the point or not).

Not all calls are 'in' or 'out'. There's also an intermediate category, usually used when a ball is good but when the caller finds this hard to accept and wants a replay:

'I just don't know.'

'I didn't see it.'

'Did you see it?'

'It looked a bit long to me, but I'm just not sure.'

'I'm sorry. I just can't call that one.'

This will be followed by a charitable invitation to 'take two' or 'play a let' (which, of course, is never quite as charitable as it sounds).

It's also worth being suspicious of players who call a ball out with a dismissive wag of the finger or shake of the head. This usually means that they can't trust their voices to lie convincingly.

Regrettably, however, lying convincingly is often what successful calling is about.

8. Who Plays Whom

'Malice is like a game of poker or tennis; you don't play it with anyone who is manifestly inferior to you'

Hilde Spiel

When our budding Racketeur first arrives at The Club, armed with his sneaky calls and sizzling (or perhaps not so sizzling) serves, his first priority will probably be to find someone to exercise them on. This is often easier said than done.

Certainly there will be a lot of people floating around with tennis rackets under their arms, not doing anything in particular, and looking as if they might like a game. Yet somehow they may not seem overeager to team up with our novice. Indeed he may have the distinct impression that whenever he so much as looks as if he's going to propose a game, the people in his vicinity start shuffling their feet and staring at the floorboards and whistling inaudibly.

This impression will almost certainly be confirmed if Our Hero, with all the genial confidence of the novice, decides to press on regardless and proposition one or two likely-looking opponents. Well, from their reaction you'd have thought he'd asked to borrow their balls, or their tennis racket, rather than play a game. And anyway, it wasn't as if Our Hero had even proposed *a proper* game. He'd simply suggested. . . 'a bit of a hit'. . . 'to fill in time'. . . 'if, of course, they had nothing better to do'. . . 'and they didn't mind teaming up with someone a bit new to the game'. Mind, it seemed, they did.

All he got was excuses – and not always very convincing ones either. 'Some other time perhaps', was about the most tactful or, 'I *think* I've got a game'. There was a distinctly condescending tone, mingled with irony, from those he took to be the better players: 'Thanks awfully for asking, but not just now. I don't think I could give anyone a decent game today.' Other claimed to be waiting for someone (even though their phantom partner never actually arrived), or to be too tired, or resting (even though they were to be seen, minutes later, taking to the field with someone else). It just didn't make sense. Why had they joined the club if they didn't want to play tennis?

To an experienced Racketeur, of course, it would make perfect sense. The question of who plays whom is no casual matter and very much determines who is who at the club. Tennis relationships are never entered into lightly.

Most good players can contemplate nothing worse than being paired up, through some ill-chance, with an unsatisfactory opponent. They will be extremely suspicious of anyone they meet socially, outside the club, who *claims* to play tennis. Until these claims have been verified, there'll be no offers, however vague, to 'have a game sometime'.

The fact is that even though ostensibly clubs are all about meeting and playing new people and there are ladders and leagues and novelty tournaments and social events to encourage this, most players prefer to stick to partners they know.

Or rather, they end up sticking to partners they know. When they start playing, things are a bit different. We all begin in tennis, as in life, searching for The Perfect Partner, someone to play the Yin to our Yang. We believe that someone somewhere has that particular blend of qualities which will combine with ours to produce the ultimate in tennis chemistry, making each game a non-stop sequence of magic moments, each match even more challenging, memorable and exciting than the last.

Our ideal opponent is someone whose game will at the same time challenge and flatter us; whose play is admired but is not so stylish that it shows us up; who is a better player but is also prepared to get beaten by us fairly regularly; whose style provides the ideal foil for all our best shots; and whose best shots (like his cracking service) are just the ones that somehow we know how to return.

But in tennis, as in life, we usually settle for less than our ideal and end up playing with a small circle of regular cronies whose failings more or less match our own.

Not that we are always content with our usual cronies. In fact most people would probably prefer to have a regular partner who is better than they are. This enhances their status (people don't like to be associated with lesser players), and improves their game. And they don't have to worry about trying to win — not usually the case when you are playing a regular partner who is about as inept as you are. (Here each meeting is likely to be a re-run of High Noon as you battle it out with no quarter given.)

Thus it is worth developing with some of your friends the sort of cosy playing relationship where you know in advance if you are going to win or lose – either because you *always* win or you *always* lose, or because you have an understanding to alternate in victory and defeat.

On the whole, though, most Racketeurs do prefer to avoid losing. It can be rather upsetting to be given a hard time by someone you clearly perceive as your inferior — frequently the case, since, as we've seen, most people believe they play better tennis than they do. As a result a good many Racketeurs seem to feel they are constantly being beaten by worse players.

It's to avoid this sort of situation that many established Racketeurs are wary of the novice. Any game with someone you don't know is going to be a battle. Only after a few matches can you settle into a steady win/lose relationship. Once such a relationship is established, incidentally, it is usually irreversible. If someone beats you three or four times, you can be sure that he will always beat you. Even if you go away for a month of special training at a tennis camp with the world's top coach things will be just the same when you get back – you may now be capable of taking a set off Jimmy Connors but you'll do no better than before against your clubmate.

It's all psychological, of course. In the same way there are certain people that your subconscious will never permit you to beat – like you best business client, or your boss. (Perhaps that's why he lets you call him by his christian name on the tennis court, though not at the office.)

But tennis clubs are not just made up of small groups of closed cliques. There are always some people at every club who are available to play all comers. It shouldn't take too long for the novice to identify those people who are prepared, *in certain circumstances*, to be picked up. The important thing is to approach them properly. Even with these people, show the proper deference, and try not to sound too competitive:

'Feel like hitting a few while you're waiting?'

'Quick set? Just to warm you up.'

Also pick your moment carefully. Avoid pouncing on people as soon as they arrive at the courts. They won't want to commit themselves to a game with you until they're sure that no one better is available. The best moment to approach them is when most potential opponents have paired off and they start to get worried that they may not get a game at all.

Your worth as an opponent, of course, is very much determined by market forces. Players who wouldn't even consider you as an opponent on Monday will go down on their knees to you on Tuesday – if they are desperate to make up a four and there's no one else around.

It's by no means true, incidentally, that people will only be reluctant to play with you if you're not good enough. There are some players (a few anyway) who have a genuine modest streak and you can put them off if you look as if you might be too good. No one wants to spend the whole game apologising.

But the matter of who plays whom is not entirely determined by relevant factors like ability and availability. Sex, for instance, can lead to some very unlikely pairings as people seek to further their prurient interests rather than their tennis.

Then there are social factors. Even people who normally stick to their own group of playing chums will make exceptions for people with whom they socialise. It can sometimes be a bit difficult to say, 'I'm your friend, but I won't play tennis with you'. There are also certain categories of people (doctors are a good example) who always seem to be able to get a game no matter how well or how badly they play.

But there is always a rather forced heartiness about such encounters, with both players working terribly hard to be sporting and give every appearance of enjoying the game. ('That *was* fun – it's nice to play someone different occasionally. You can get stuck in such a rut always playing the same old people. We must do it again at some stage.') You can be sure, however, that the experiment will not be repeated too often.

There are also a certain number of key figures at *every* club with whom we all feel an obligation to play if they indicate that they'd like a game. These are often members of the club's official heirarchy – like the President (who is normally selected for his supposed distinction rather than his playing ability), or one of the committee members, or perhaps the person who donated the new club notice board, or the venerable ancient who captained the team 40 years before.

These people are far from ideal partners, and are often, at best, extremely rusty. But because of their status they usually get their way. So you and your fellow Racketeurs will invite them to play, and will *pretend* to be enjoying the game and will *seem* not to notice when, say, every other point in a doubles match is lost by the Man of Distinction. Even the Man of Distinction's partner can be counted on to grit his teeth and smile bravely. (In similar circumstances our novice Racketeur would, of course, be made only too aware of his inadequacies.)

But playing with these people is not too onerous a duty since it's not that often that they get the urge, preferring to assert themselves in the clubhouse rather than on the court (of which, more anon).

9. Club Classes

'Gentlemen are requested not to play in their shirt sleeves when ladies are present'

Notice on Club Secretary's Board at the original Worple Road club, Wimbledon (now Wimbledon Girl's High School)

Some people, like our Rising Racketeur join the club to play tennis. Others play tennis simply in order to join the club. It could be any club. They will spend most of their time their indulging in some other activity. This may be another sport, such as playing cards, darts or ping pong. Or it may be a social activity like gossiping or drinking or wife-swapping. Or it may be *organising.*

Tennis clubs offer a good deal of scope for life's organisers and they tend to be among the most prominent members in the heirarchy of any tennis club.

Few members enjoy the same sort of status as the key organisers – except possibly for one or two exceptionally gifted players and a few other people with somewhat less valid claims to distinction, like being rich, attractive or famous. And as titular head, of course, there's always the Club President – someone with a bit of a name who can represent the club and can arbitrate, when necessary, between factions.

But when it comes down to the nitty gritty of club power, the Politburo par excellence is The Committee. It's here that you will find nature's bureaucrats holding their interminable meetings, allocating functions to one another and ever concerned, in everyone's best interests, naturally, to regulate the habits and behaviour of everyone else. They meet frequently – once a year inviting the rest of the club along for the Annual General Meeting – and post the results of their labours on the club notice boards:

'Members are reminded that Court Six on alternate Tuesdays between 7.30 and 9.30 pm is reserved for Under Threes Team Practice.'

'The Groundsman has asked members to be especially vigilant when turning on the hose on the outer courts since careless use has been causing flooding in the basements of nearby houses.'

'Mr Jones, who occupies the house alongside Court Eight, has informed The Club that he has electrified his fence to prevent members from climbing into his garden to look for lost balls.'

'The club rules on clothing have been amended (by a narrow majority) to permit striped gear, provided that it is proper tennis apparel. Rugby shirts are not permitted. In view of the strong feelings aroused by this issue, the Committee will review the situation again in a year's time.'

'To prevent a recurrence of the ugly scenes which occurred recently involving some members and the Deputy Coach over the use of Court Five, it has been decided that this court will now be designated as the Spare Coaching Court. The

Assistant Coach will have priority on this court on weekday evenings every other week from 6 to 10 pm.'

'Members are reminded that club rules require members playing singles to double up *immediately* at the designated peak periods. There is no rule, and never has been, which permits them to finish off the set first. Members who fail to comply should be reported to the Committee.'

'Miss Cook has been named Secretary of the Catering Sub-Committee.'

'Mr Stretcher has been authorised to offer to members his services as a racket stringer following his successful completion of the Racket Stringing Association Advanced Proficiency Examination (Part Two).'

These last two notices handing out sinecures show one of the ways in which the Committee perpetuates its power.

The main recipients of committee patronage are the groundsman and the club coach. They depend on the club for their living. Only in the name of the Committee can the coach keep rival coaches off his patch and deal with other threats to his livelihood – like talented juniors offering cut price lessons or stringing rackets on the side.

Allied to the Committee there will be a supporting team of lesser officials, willing busybodies who are only too glad to allow themselves to be co-opted for various tasks, and, in turn, to co-opt others. They keep themselves busy organising the club dance or barbecue or ladder or league or duty rota or handicap tournament and spend a good deal of time sitting on assorted ad hoc (in practice almost permanent) sub-committees – The Bar Committee, The Team Selection Committee, The Disco Decorating Committee, The New Court Committee, The Memorial Cup Fund-Raising Committee and so on.

These people may also play tennis occasionally if no one else can be found to make up a four – they do usually bring their gear along. But their main pleasure comes from putting other people together – making up fours of people who hate each other; or organising silly tournaments (Round Robin, Husband and Wife, Father and Son, Three-a-side, Piggy Back, American, Novice and Expert, Left-handed) – again giving people who dislike each other the opportunity to meet (no real way out here since if you don't play in the silly tournaments you can't get a court); or organising children in some particularly noisy activity (also bound to take up a lot of court space); or generally wandering around being hearty, selling raffle tickets and trying to press you into service or at least secure your support for some forthcoming event.

One common characteristic of these people is that they are usually rather jolly. This is not the case with Full Members of the Committee, who are presumably weighed down by their responsibilities. Full Members are often seen in pairs, walking around deep in earnest conversation, only occasionally breaking off to ask when they spot someone they don't recognise: 'Is that chap a member?' Committee Members are rarely seen wielding a racket. The tennis bag has been swapped for the brief case. And although they say they'd *love* to spend more time on court, their duties don't seem to allow them the time.

Should you point out that they do seem to rather *enjoy* their duties, you'll be told they would gladly step down if someone else was willing to take over. The only reason, they say defensively, that it's always the same old people on the committee is that no one else ever volunteers.

These bureaucrats then are people at the top of the social pyramid that makes up the club, along with one or two classy Racketeurs — the sort of players who point at the ball as they prepare to smash their overheads and who pick up the ball by patting it with the middle of their rackets so that it b-b-bounces up.

It's in the middle levels that you find the majority of average Racketeurs. The game, of course, is their main interest, but unlike the classy Racketeurs they tend to have a few complexes about it. They fear rather than look forward to making an overhead smash. And when they pick up the ball it's by flicking it up with their racket against the side of their shoe rather than with the deft p-p-pat of the pro.

These middle levels will also contain a good many non-players, or at least non-players of tennis. There'll be plenty of players of *other* sports like darts or ping pong. These people use the club mainly as a source of partners for their other activities. They're the sort who in the middle of a standard Racketeur conversation will suddenly change tack and ask:

'I say, you don't play bridge, do you?'

Other non-players will be looking for business contacts or quite simply clients – they may want to sell you insurance or tile your bathroom.

But perhaps the worst sort of non-players are those for whom the club is a sort of refuge – from their spouse, children or work. They are the ones who spend the longest hours there, usually at the bar, most of the time reminiscing. An awful lot of their conversations start off with: 'Do you remember old. . .?' They are also great ailment swappers and know exactly what everyone in the club is suffering from and what they should do about it. Whenever a member snuffs it, it's: 'What did I tell you?'

The doyen of this non-playing group is usually someone once prominent in club life but now retired or convalescing. He features in one of the old team pictures on the wall, and is still upset that for the last five years he's no longer been called on to referee the main club tournament. He tends to judge people by how long they've been members but he'll even be prepared to indulge his nostalgia with a comparative newcomer – if no one else can be found (frequently the case).

The base of the club pyramid is reserved for the 'untouchables' – social outcasts or rotten players. These are often newcomers who are going to have to serve a long apprenticeship on the outside courts, trading their double hits and bucket shots (which they, incidentally, count as good). As part of the learning process they will at intervals be bellowed at by some enraged Committee Member:

'Will you turn that sprinkler off immediately please.'

'May I suggest you read the Club Rules about weekend play.'

'Kindly put your shirt on. This is a tennis club not the public park.'

The relative size of each group, of course, varies a good deal from club to club. The long established, wood-panelled sort of club with a long waiting list is likely to be rather top-heavy with officials and older people who were something in the game *once*.

The young club which is short of funds and needs money for a new court or clubhouse will probably have a large proportion of 'untouchables'.

The suburban club used mainly by weekenders is likely to have more than its fair share of busy bees organising barbecues, punch-and-paté parties, discos and novelty tournaments and urging everyone else to participate ('Now, John, what can we ask you to do?').

The in-town pay-and-play club (perhaps with sauna and health studios attached) will usually be more like an American Racquet club, run by full time staff rather than by amateur organisers. They may even provide you with balls, though you will, of course, pay for them in the end – through the nose.

But what ever sort of club you choose, the first lesson is to know your place. If you don't you'll soon be shown it.

10. Doubles

**'The duration record for doubles is 84hr 7 min by
Daryl Murray, Richard Munao, Stephen Duerden and
Stephen Foord at the Racquet Centre, Silverwater,
NSW, Australia on 7-10 Jan 1980'**

Guiness Book of Records 1983

Everyone thinks tennis is about singles. Club Racketeurs know that because of the shortage of courts, and shortage of wind, too, for that matter, it's mainly about doubles – especially at weekends.

Doubles ought to be a friendly gathering of friends. Isn't that why you learned to play tennis in the first place – to meet people and have fun in the open air? But it's more likely to resemble an alfresco encounter group – with all the attendant tensions and traumas.

Foursomes do have their advantages. There's someone to blame when things go wrong. You can also conceal your lack of condition. And doubles does offer the most scope for the Racketeur intellectual since it's all about talking and tactics and diplomacy and deviousness.

It is also more complicated. Instead of having one person to cope with, you have three. Don't assume that the one on your side will be the easiest to handle.

We've already seen how difficult it is to match up just two tennis egos. Putting four together poses a lot more problems. This is why many foursomes, once they've found a combination that works, make it into a regular thing. You never quite know what you're letting yourself in for with 'accidental' foursomes.

When you've got your four together the big question is Who Plays with Whom, i.e. who is the greatest asset and who is the greatest liability. It's as well at this point, to get your oar in first. Don't be too obvious about it by straightaway putting your arm round the best player and claiming him or her as your partner. There are subtler ways of saying the same thing: 'Let's try it this way – A and B against C and me. If it doesn't work we can always swap round'.

It's important to get the right partner, since your relationship is likely to be the single most important factor in determining the outcome of the game.

There can be a problem right from the start over who takes charge. If one player is clearly superior, it's easier. But if you are not agreed on who should take the left box (rightly or wrongly, the Status Side) and who should call the shots, the battle on your side of the net is likely to be more intense than the battle across it.

Of course, you'll never find the ideal partner, just as you'll never find the ideal opponent. But here are some types to avoid:

THE CAPTAIN

Will immediately assume stewardship of your team, even though his leadership qualities and superior abilities may not be all that obvious to you. He'll elect to serve first, unless, of course, he doesn't like serving into the sun or the wind. If things start going wrong he'll keep giving you orders and calling you over for tactical talks. It wouldn't be so bad if he took the blame when you lose, but in that event, of course, it'll all be your fault.

THE COACH

This partner also assumes a superiority which is not exactly self-evident. Most of his time will be spent giving you advice — to start with, perhaps, in a benign avuncular manner:

'Try standing in a bit nearer when you're receiving, old son.'

'Come on, bend your knees.'

'Now then, remember what I told you. Keep your racket head up.'

If you don't accept these friendly admonitions, he may become a bit sterner or adopt an even more patronising 'things only your best friend would tell you' approach. The only effect of all this will be to reduce your standard of play as you seethe with indignation and concentrate on deliberately *not* bending your knees.

THE TRAITOR

Also irritatingly patronising with plenty to say about your game. Most of his remarks about you are made to the opposition:

'Don't you wish you had a partner like mine?'

'How does he do it?' (when you hit a loose one).

'You wouldn't like him on your side, would you?'

'When can we swap round?'

The nearest he'll come to giving useful advice will be something like:

'Nice shot, wrong court' (another of your loose shots).

'You paid a lot for that racket. Why not use all of it' (when you come off the wood).

But even this sort of remark will be made with a wink to the opposition. You may be forgiven for wondering whose side he is on.

THE FLATTERER

Also has a lot to say to the opposition – at his own team's expense. Is forever telling *them* what great shots *they're* playing, how well they work together, how they're not giving *your* team a chance. There's nothing subtle about this. It's not a ploy to boost their morale and make them overconfident. He's simply the type that always appeases the enemy – and a born loser on the tennis court.

THE COMMENTATOR

Much of the art of doubles is skilful chitchat. But this man has too much to say. There'll be a long monologue after every point, summing up the situation, explaining where you went wrong and advising you on tactics. His speciality is offering useless advice at key moments:

'Important point to win, partner' (when you're receiving serve).

'OK. This is where we hit them' (when you're being outplayed on every point).

'We've got them on the run partner' (usually wishful thinking, rather than a statement of fact).

THE POINT-AWARDER

This partner doesn't just lavish praise on the opposition, he gives them points as well – *your* points. It's *your* serves that he calls out – before the opposition have even said a word (*he* can see because he's up at the net). When you've received serve and are about to call it out, he's asking the server to 'Take Two' (*he* can see because he's alongside the service line). When you return serve with a fantastic winner and everyone starts changing over, *he* lets it be known that the serve was out. It's all designed to show what a great sportsman he is. The trouble is it's at *your* expense.

THE WASTREL

Also determined to show what a big-hearted player he is, diminishing his partner in the process. As you scramble and scrounge for points, he merrily squanders any advantage by playing double or quits – carelessly slamming the ball out of court and trying ambitious shots that don't come off. If he can't win big, he'd rather not win at all. If you dare suggest that it might be better just to poop the ball over instead of double-faulting all the time, he'll reply:

'I came to play tennis, not pat-a-cake.'

'It's only a game you know.'

'Don't take it all so seriously.'

THE FALLING STAR

A close cousin. This player has been in a few big games in his time but is now coming down in the tennis world. Thus, he's rather contemptuous of the other three people on court and feels, mistakenly, they should be grateful he's playing with them at all. His main concern will be to use the match as a means of getting his own game back into gear rather than to help his partner win the match. When he's not hitting his Big but Bad shots out of court, he'll be kicking the net and cursing ('I don't believe it') and threatening to give the game up for ever (vain hope).

THE SLUMMER

A similar sort, but less of a *prima donna*, and a better player. He, too, feels this foursome is a bit of a come-down, but he believes there's no harm in playing with the lower orders once in a while, and they do *so appreciate it*. He usually remains aloof throughout, too much of a tennis gent to curse or criticise when his partner commits a no-no. But his contempt will be thinly disguised. He may not say anything when his partner flubs but there'll be a 'some mothers do have 'em' sort of sigh as he ambles into position for the next point.

THE SOLOIST

Another player with little regard for his partner's ego. Is always poaching, shouting 'Mine' or 'Leave' and trying to cover three-quarters of the court by himself. He sees your job as trying to do as little damage as possible ('You cover the alley and keep 'em honest') while he plays for both of you. Has an irritating habit of looking back at you when you serve, or even more humiliating, retreating to the baseline for your second serve. This may, of course, be self-defence, but still it's not very polite.

THE TACTICIAN

Someone once told this player that doubles was about tactics. So he's forever coming over for a tactical huddle, proposing schemes that are far too ambitious for either of you to bring off, and making incomprehensible hand signals behind his back whenever you're serving. He'll suddenly suggest switching to the Australian formation (which neither of you has practised) 'to confuse the opposition' (you are the ones that get confused). Or he'll insist you play 'two up' when neither of you can volley. When you're serving, he'll look back and whisper 'Hit to his backhand with lots of top' (the best you are hoping for is to get it over the net and into the box). The only thing to do is nod and agree and then play your usual game. He won't notice the difference.

THE-STATER-OF-THE-OBVIOUS

Also has plenty to say, but nothing of any use and nothing that isn't already abundantly clear to all concerned. Has a happy knack of stating the obvious, usually with some solemnity, in the belief that he's imparting great truths to his partner:

'Wait for it.'
'We've got to win this point to stay in the game.'
'If you win your serve, we're in business.'
'It's up to you to try to win your serve.'

THE MIND CHANGER

Another very vocal player. His speciality is giving instructions and then contradicting himself:

'Mine. . . no, yours.'
'Up. . . sorry, back, back.'
'Leave. . . OK, you take it.'
'Let's go now. . . no, wait for it.'

If he tells you the ball's going out, you can be sure it'll land in. If he tells you to let it bounce, you'll be better off hitting it first time.

THE CONFUSER

A close cousin, who can create even more chaos. As well as issuing contradictory instructions, this player will always be swapping sides, changing his mind about who should do what, serving from the wrong box and muddling up the score. You will frequently bash rackets with this partner as you collide in mid-court and go after the same balls.

THE APOLOGISER

Is forever apologising ('Sorry', 'Silly me', 'My mistake') lamenting what a rotten partner he is and saying he doesn't know how you put up with him ('Look, if you'd rather stop, just say the word'). It's nice of him to admit he goofed ('My fault') but he's not saying anything everyone else doesn't know. Who else's fault could it be when he fails to return service? You rather wish he'd save his energy for getting the ball back. Also has a habit of explaining what went wrong after each muffed shot. ('I'm just not stepping into my shots properly. Am I ever going to learn?')

THE POOPER

The opposite of the poacher. This player just can't seem to bring himself to put the ball away. Doubles for him seems to be all about keeping the ball in play. If he's at the net and gets given an easy smash to kill – a sitter that you've both worked hard to set up – he'll probably just poop it back to the opposition ('Didn't want to risk anything at this stage, partner').

THE POACHER

Not a bad partner if he brings it off. Usually, of course, he doesn't – he just lunges hopelessly at every cross-court ball, putting you off your stroke as you try to return. Tends to stand so near the middle when you're serving that you're frightened to hit him in the back. *His* alley, of course, is left for you to protect. Even if his success rate is only one in twenty, he'll carry on regardless ('Sorry, partner, but I thought it was worth a try').

THE BALL-BOY

Likes to keep all the balls on your side of the court. Even when the opposition are serving, he'll ration their supply (although there's absolutely no perceivable advantage to be gained from this). He'll always have two or three balls in his pockets. When *you're* serving, he'll reluctantly provide you with a couple of balls either from his pocket or from the little collection in front of him at the net.

So much for what to avoid. But what should you look *for* in a doubles partner?

Ideally, you need someone who can play a bit and to whom you are happy to defer as team-leader. In return he should support, rather than suffer you, as a partner. And he should let you play a bit, too. There's nothing worse than a game where the two stars on either side bat it back and forth, making it clear that the less the other two players have to do with it, the better.

The ideal partner knows how to encourage his mate with frequent shouts of 'Good shot' and 'Well played', *particularly when the opposition look doubtful.*

In the event that your opponents do have the gall to call any of your winners out, you and your ideal partner will have perfected the art of looking quizzically at one another and thus putting the opposition to shame.

If any lobbying should be necessary to get your shot called in, you can count on your ideal partner to do it for you. Indeed, he works up as much righteous indignation about injustices against *you* as against himself.

When you, perchance, perform a dirty deed calling the opposition out when perhaps they don't quite deserve it, you can count on total solidarity from your ideal partner when you ask him innocently:

'What did you think, partner?'

He will then proceed to lie with conviction, not cop out and say he didn't see it.

If something goes wrong with one of your better shots, your ideal partner will be sympathetic and encouraging, explaining how difficult such shots are to get hold of:

'One of the trickiest shots in the book, that one – and there was a lot of disguised spin on the ball.'

'We may not be winning, but we're showing 'em a thing or two.'

The ideal partner poaches at the right moments, puts away the shots you set up and does not double-fault.

The ideal partner knows the score at all times, and if he should make a mistake it's in your team's favour.

Your ideal partner and you have an almost telepathic understanding of how best to upset the opposition – instinctively choosing the right moments to create a diversion or touch off a dispute.

However badly you play, the ideal partner always says he wants to play with you again – even if he doesn't really mean it.

Rules of Tennis

SELF-KNOWLEDGE

Not everyone who 'plays tennis' really can.

80 per cent of tennis players consider themselves above average.

All Racketeurs believe themselves better players than they actually are.

Most Racketeurs play better at the bar, or in their mind's eye, or while watching others, than they do on court.

Most Racketeurs find it easier to spot the faults in someone else's game than in their own.

Every Racketeur has some advice for every other Racketeur.

The worst players have the most advice to give.

The stranger you give advice to in the bar will turn out to be twice as good as you are.

People with all the best gear don't always have a game to match.

All Racketeurs worry about their backhands.

---

11. Mixed Doubles

**'I've had distemper and I've played mixed doubles . . .
I'd rather have distemper'**
Snoopy

Some men players, chauvinists that they are, automatically become very suspicious if someone comes up and asks them whether they'd like to make up a four. They suspect it may be an invitation to play mixed doubles. As often as not, they are right.

Not that there's anything wrong, exactly, with playing mixed doubles, you understand. This is when tennis is supposed to be the most fun, when winning is not really important. In fact, 'hit and giggle' games are no joke. On the tennis courts, the battle of the sexes can be at its keenest, domestic warfare at its most intense.

Nevertheless, few people manage to avoid 'mixed troubles' entirely. Even those who believe that the sexual/social side of tennis is best left to the clubhouse find themselves playing the game from time to time – especially at weekends.

The main problem with mixed doubles, let it be said at the start, is the male tennis ego. We've already seen how people parade their egos on the tennis court. No surprise, then, that the male ego should be at its most prickly when playing tennis with the female of the species. In fact when playing mixed doubles most men resemble one or other of the highly avoidable partner-types described in the previous chapter.

The man will, for instance, immediately assume captainship of the side. Even when the woman is the better player, he is never in any doubt about who should lead the team and give the orders. He is, after all, bigger and stronger and can hit the ball harder. What more need be said?

Needless to say, this arrangement doesn't always reflect real abilities – especially in a country like England where many women have a better tennis education than men as a result of being taught the game at school.

The other assumption the man will make is that his female partner is in need of instruction – *his* instruction. Many men will, without hesitation, set about remodelling a woman's whole game in the course of two sets of doubles – regardless of whether this may or may not be necessary, and regardless of his qualifications for the task. At the very least, the man will assume the role of Counsellor and Tactician.

The woman really has two choices. She can grin and bear it – probably the best way of furthering her team's chances in the match. Or she can resist – which may not help her team but may do something for women's rights on the tennis court.

Racketeuses who are not prepared to let things pass should beware of two main enemies – men who *poach* and men who *coach*.

The poachers view mixed doubles as a game between two men with two women on hand to decorate the court and lead the cheering. They pig every ball and are forever shouting: 'Mine', 'OK', 'Leave', 'I've got it', 'I'm there', 'I'll handle it', 'Lemme take it', and words to that effect. The woman will be given an alley to look after (woe betide her if she fails to protect *that*) and the man will do the rest. Her only other function – perhaps more important from the man's point of view – is to admire and applaud the antics of her partner.

The coacher will let the woman play a bit more but only to enable him to work on her game. Her *every* move will give rise to criticism or advice. However she plays the ball, he'll suggest another way:

'Try and take it a bit earlier, pet.'

'That's better, but you're still slicing. Try the topspin like I showed you.'

Any recalcitrance by the woman may cause him to become rather more severe:

'Come on, girl, move!'

'Hit the ball.'

Failure by the woman to perform as instructed will lead to frequent 'what can you do with them' looks across the net to the other male on court.

The main occasion for dispensing advice will be when the woman serves:

'Toss the ball higher, love.'

Rules of Tennis

SERVING

There are two kinds of server – those who hold the second ball in their hand and those who don't.

The complexity of the wind-up will bear no relation to the quality of the serve.

All your best serves will be returned or called out.

You will call your opponent's best serves out.

Happiness is a service that clips the service line and gets called in.

When a player didn't see an opponent's serve, he will frequently go over and point at the spot where it landed.

It's the mishits and marshmallows that are most likely to be outright winners.

Players with big first serves often have to use their second.

The more important the point, the more times you will bounce the ball.

You always double-fault when you can least afford to.

No one serves like he thinks he serves.

'Now remember to follow through this time.'

'You forgot to scratch your back again, didn't you?'

The woman may find it harder to defend herself here as service is often the weakest part of her game. But she can always point out that at least her pastry puff serves are an improvement on her partner's double-faults.

Men, of course, have their own version of the mixed doubles story.

Women, they will say, want it all ways – to be treated as equals and at the same time to receive special consideration, to call the shots but not to have to serve into the wind or the sun.

Many men feel that however hard they try, it's impossible to do the right thing by their partner. If they invite her to serve first, they're accused of being patronising. If they serve first, they're ungallant.

If the woman stands in too close and receives a cannonball, her partner will be blamed for not warning her. At other times if he so much as clears his throat he'll find the woman staring daggers at him or snapping:

'You play your game and I'll play mine.'

And not only does the man have to cope with his partner. There's also the woman on the other side of the net to worry about.

Even though the basic aim of tennis is to make life difficult for the opposition, in mixed doubles the man is supposed to do this *without being beastly to the woman opposite.*

When he serves to her, it must be neither too fast (unfair) nor too slow (patronising and offensive). His serve must be *just so*.

If he hits the ball mainly at the other man, he's accused of being piggish and keeping the other woman out of the game. Yet if he hits to the other woman, he's accused of taking advantage of the weaker player.

Tactics that he's spent years developing – like luring the opposition into the net with a deft drop shot and then smashing the ball to their feet – are branded as underhand and inconsiderate. In fact it's almost impossible to play a shot to a woman at the net (not usually her preferred position) that will meet with approval. Some males favour a technique of smashing towards the woman while expressing great concern for her safety, but this is not usually appreciated either.

Despite these problems, however, you are still better off playing *against* rather than *with* someone you love. Very few marriages can survive regular tennis with one's spouse as *partner*. Even though he or she may at first feel slighted if the other won't play with him/her in the tournament, in the end it's in the best interests of both parties.

Things are different, of course, when sex, rather than tennis, is the main aim of the exercise. Doubles can be an ideal way of becoming better acquainted with John or Joan Hunter Dunn, 'furnish'd and burnish'd by Aldershot sun'.

Indeed, mixed doubles does have a perhaps undeserved reputation for being a prelude to all kinds of sexual goings on. Certainly the arrival of 'Swinging Singles Tennis Clubs' in America would seem to indicate that the game is seen as a good way of getting people together.

Some American clubs even organise so-called 'musical' tennis on Special Swingers Nights. Foursomes become sixsomes (three men and three women) so that two players can always be sidelined to enable them to get to know one another better.

'Getting to know you' games do, however, tend to lead to behaviour that is, to say the least, somewhat eccentric for mixed doubles: you find partners behaving terribly sweetly to one another. A woman's inability to return service will be thought absolutely charming by her partner. A man's advice and instruction will earn his partner's enthusiastic appreciation.

In fact those people who see doubles mainly as a way of furthering their prurient interests, would probably do better to forget the tennis and devote themselves completely to *après*-tennis. (Or adopting Jean Borotra's technique of lunging for wide balls into the lap of the most attractive woman spectator.) Many people with a trim pair of calves and a winning way with a tennis racket find that they can make better use of these assets in the clubhouse than on court. If anything, actually playing probably reduces rather than enhances sex-appeal. The state in which most people come off court – red-faced, sweating and distraught – is not usually all that becoming. And anyway all those hours slogging away on court don't really leave you in the best of shape for those après-tennis activities.

12. Wimbledon

'The British would pack Centre Court to watch two rabbits play Wimbledon'

Jack Kramer

Even though Racketeurs spend most of their time battling away at their local club, they also manage to fit in a number of major tournaments. One that we all find time for is 'The Championships' — Wimbledon (otherwise known to American commentators as Wimbleton or The Big W). Like Snoopy, we all catch the District Line tube to Southfields every year – in spirit, anyway.

It's at such big tournaments that many Racketeurs excel. It's surprising how many of us seem to have a talent for vicarious tennis. Not that we're mere onlookers, doing our playing through our favourite superstars. Make no mistake, we're also out there playing, and frequently making rather a better job of it, as we sit in front of the TV casually flicking backhands down the line past some of the world's top players.

How often we find that Yannick or Tracy could make life so much easier for themselves if they'd simply follow our advice? It's amazing that they should fail to spot so many straight winners that are so obvious to us. And yet they *will* keep on playing *crosscourt* when they should be going *down the line* and *following the ball in*.

It's hardly surprising therefore that many Racketeurs find themselves wondering how some of the big names should have made it to the top, while their own talents go unrecognised even at the local club.

They often suspect it may be something to do with the level at which the game is played. Clearly, many Racketeurs who have a hard time holding on to their humble place on the club ladder, just aren't playing the game at their natural level, i.e. Wimbledon. Now, if they were out there on Centre Court, it would be a different story, a very different story. On reflection, however, many Racketeurs will admit that even though they have one of the finest tennis brains around, it's the superstars who perhaps have the arms and legs for the game. And, on the whole, they're happy enough to let the pros get on with it. It's what they're paid for, after all. And in fact, every one of those young performers is really just playing for us, for the rest of tenniskind. They're simply the distillation of the talent that the rest of us contribute to the world's tennis pool.

Not that we don't all daydream occasionally. There's not a Racketeur anywhere who, come Wimbledon, doesn't have a vision of himself, with a bunch of rackets under his arm, striding out onto Centre Court, musing on Kipling's inscription ('If you can meet with triumph and disaster. . .'). There'll be a glance up at the scoreboard bearing your name and *initials* – it's J.S. Connors, at Wimbledon, not Jimmy. And then you'll casually set about trading balls with your opponent until that pregnant moment when the umpire will peer down from his high chair and ask:

'Are you ready? Play.'

So what is Wimbledonitis, this mysterious disease, which, for two hay-feverish weeks a year ('The Fortnight') affects the whole of Britain and amongst Racketeers the world over replaces tennis elbow as the prevailing affliction?

For one thing, it's where we pay our annual homage to the Gods of tennis. Rightly or wrongly (there are plenty of versions about the true origins of the game) we see those ivy-clad walls in SW19 as the true temple of tennis. And now that the brown grass of Forest Hills has been abandoned for the synthetic greenery (Deco-turf II) of Flushing Meadows, the All England Lawn Tennis and Croquet Club seems to stand even more alone.

These are the original Strawberry fields – a sort of English garden party to which

Rules of Tennis

POINTSCORING

A call is not so much a statement of fact as a bargaining position.

'Just out' often means 'just in'.

When in doubt, most Racketeers call it out.

The more doubtful you are, the more certain you will sound.

There's nothing at all definite about a ball that's called 'definitely in' or 'definintely out'.

The balls you say you saw most clearly are the ones you didn't see at all.

You're at your most generous with points when you're well ahead or well behind.

If you are disturbed during play by a ball from another court, whether or not you say 'take two' will depend on who wins the point.

You are more likely to win a point by mishitting, or by coming off the wood, than you are by playing a good shot.

Whenever you're sure you've hit a winner, it'll be returned.

The best winners are the ones you never expected to land in court.

When you're 3 – 0 up in the first set, you won't believe your luck will last.

When you're 0 – 3 down, you'll worry that you might not get a game at all.

Passers-by only ask you the score when you're losing.

the rest of the tennis world is invited. It may have got a bit bigger since the first championships was held at Worple Road with 200 people watching and *The Times* devoting 10 lines to the event, but it's still a select gathering of tennis folk.

At least, that's what we like to believe. In practice, it's not quite that select. Most of us are *not* guests in the Members' Enclosure, nor do we mingle with the stars in the competitors' lounge, nor even get invited to champagne and smoked salmon in one of the sponsored marquees.

You can, of course, bring your own bottle of bubbly and picnic in the car park. And there are still those Bath buns and famous strawberry and cream teas. Every year seems to set a new record for how much you can charge for six squashy strawberries. But somehow those carefully measured punnets which now compete with Scotch eggs, chocolate éclairs, lollies, hot dogs and *hamburgers,* all consumed in a crush amid the litter of cans and paper cups, don't seem quite what they were. These days it's more likely to be the fragrance of frying onions, rather than the scent of Wimbledon's pink and blue hydrangeas that wafts up to the Royal Box.

It's also likely to be a battle to get there in the first place – the crush on the tube, and then the long slog from the station, unless you want to get ripped off by a taxi. On arrival, there's the endless queue, constantly menaced by pick-pockets and scalpers (don't part with your tenners till you get your fingers round the tickets). And when you do get inside you probably won't be able to see anything as you wander round the outside courts catching a glimpse of the occasional high lob and the steeple of St Mary's church. Still, even if you spent most of your afternoon milling around and queuing, you will have been to *Wimbledon.*

If you are fortunate enough to have a seat, your neighbours are no longer likely to be the traditional pink-cheeked white-whiskered English gent, in blazer and flannels, accompanied by his good lady in a floppy hat with fruit on top. You are more likely to be sitting next to some bejeaned youth from Akron, Ohio, decked out in Wimbledon souvenir hat, badges and pennants, who spent the night outside in a sleeping bag and whose main aim is to add to his souvenir collection one of those notices so prized in America, warning that 'only ten minutes are allowed for knocking up'. (This apparently means something *very different* over there.)

Instead of politely clapping, your fellow spectators these days are more likely to go in for the near-riotous whistling, wailing and whooping that used to be confined to the Foro Italico in Rome. And it will all be unashamedly partisan, not in the Wimbledon tradition of even-handed support, always trying to give a bit of a lift to the underdog.

And yet, things don't seem to have changed so much. Somehow even Wimbledon noise does manage to remain that little bit classier. Nothing else quite resembles the sound of tennis balls being struck on Centre Court or the interruptions from the walkway above No. 1 Court. And there is still a sense of it all being an English family affair – still run, of course, by the same exclusive self-perpetuating oligarchy of Members (the ones with the green and mauve neckties, who continue to make a fortune out of the small fortune that we hand over to the ticket touts).

It doesn't seem so long ago that all the prizes were carved up by three English families – the Renshaws, the Baddeleys and those Doherty brothers who never even used to roll up their sleeves. And English Racketeers still seem to feel there's no reason why some unseeded local hero shouldn't emerge from nowhere to win the singles. Perhaps someone like P. Frank Hadow, the coffee planter, who taught himself the game by hitting against a wall in Ceylon, came back to England to win the singles in 1878, and then returned to Ceylon, never seeing another game till he returned at the age of 71 to watch the 1926 finals.

Admittedly hopes of such heroes today are something of a triumph of optimism over experience. Despite the liberal distribution of 'wild cards' to British non-entities to encourage 'home interest', home grown stars, even if they occasionally flatter in the early rounds, tend only to deceive later on. In the end our Golden Boys and Girls never quite rise to the occasion. Nevertheless that sardonic line in a West End play ('I hear Virginia's doing very well at Wimbledon this year') which seemed to have the ring of truth about it at the time, did get its comeuppance in the end.

Despite it all, however, Wimbledon still manages every year to hold a nation in its grip. There's nothing else on television, and little else in the newspapers, as journalists battle it out, trading cross-court clichés, Delphic predictions, statements of the obvious and making passing shots at Jimbo and Superbrat ('Will it be another Jimbledon?' 'Will this be the year that MacTantrum gets thrown out of the tournament?'). The country's supply of strawberries is diverted to SW19. People wander round wearing tennis visors and carrying tennis rackets. And when it's all over they all take to the courts (most for the only time of the year) to indulge in a sort of English Midsummer orgy of awful tennis.

But it's not just the British who think that Wimbledon is rather special. The rest of the tennis world seems to as well. Where else can anyone possibly know quite so much about grass (exactly 3/16th of an inch high)? What other tournament has so many delightful oddities – the giant roller that cannot be moved from Centre Court, the Robinsons Barley Water with the label always turned towards camera, the eccentric seedings and strange decisions by the Order-of-Play Committee. There's also the charm of those dozy linesmen (who will have the distinction of wrong-calling in front of 200 million people) and those umpires calling 30 – 40 instead of 40 – 30 and gravely mispronouncing those foreign names. And then there's all the fun and games provided by the regular conflicts between Players and The Committee, and the annual controversies over No.2 Court.

Fnally, of course, there's the weather, which tends to provide the real drama at Wimbledon. The only thing you can really be sure of at Wimbledon is that it will rain. As Pat Dupre said one year, 'Its always either rainy with sunny intervals or sunny with rainy intervals'. So will we spend our afternoons watching tennis or will the cameras remain focused on those pools of water on the court covers? Will we actually get through the programme in two weeks? Will the grass stand up to it? And how many more times will our favourite commentators explain to us the significance of the service break, *and the even greater importance of breaking back quickly*?

But despite it all, Wimbledon remains, as *Time* magazine once said, 'except for the monarchy, Britain's most successful institution', and despite the arrival of so many things that aren't quite Wimbledon – the sale of John McEnroe self-confidence cassettes, betting tents, electronic 'Cyclops' line monitors, net-cord judges with earphones, Leyland saloons instead of limousines to ferry the players around, and perhaps, one day, the unthinkable, artificial grass — Wimbledon has managed to remain Wimbledon, just.

13. Tennis Watching

'For the rules of toilet tennis, see opposite wall'
'For the rules of toilet·tennis, see opposite wall'

Graffiti, on opposite walls of a public lavatory in Wimbledon

Tennis-watching is as much an acquired art as tennis-playing and any self-respecting Racketeer must spend some time developing his skills. Essentially, of course, this means tennis talk. Even if you can't play, there's no reason why you shouldn't excel as a commentator. Here are a few tips:

Always talk about top level tennis as if it's very much on a par with your own, as if the superstars were your daily sparring parners. Use of their nicknames ('Rocket', 'Jimbo', 'Chrissie', 'Ginny') is one way of conveying this familiarity.

Don't hesitate to pass judgement and criticise. That's what the stars are there for – to give the rest of us someone to watch and pontificate about. It's when discussing the champions that you can afford to be at your most patronising and dismissive:

'Of course, Borg did get so much better at the net, but he never managed to tidy up that backhand volley.'

Be familiar with the stars' little weaknesses (Denton's tendency to overhit under pressure, Wilander's second service, Vilas' excessive backlift and Connors' return of a heavily sliced serve). These people have their failings too – just as you have your difficulties at hitting backhands that don't sail out of court.

Respect or reverence should only be reserved for the Golden Greats, i.e. any of the big names BC (Before Connors). These are the players *you* identify with. After all, you've been around a while too, and you've seen a lot of tennis. At least that's the impression you want to give. And you're not sure the game will *ever* again see the likes of Budge's backhand, Kramer's forehand, Laver's topspin lob, Rosewall's footwork, Hoad's forehand volley or Santana's backspin dropshot.

Any claims by a rival commentator that one of today's stars has a lightning fast serve, and you dismiss them with Gonzales or Sangster. Any assertions that yesterday's men couldn't handle today's fast net-rushing game, and you weigh in with Borotra.

The accomplished tennis watcher has seen it all before and knows that there's never anything new in tennis. No opportunity will be lost to cite some pertinent parallel from the past. He can even remember the scores in many of the great encounters of yesteryear and can tell you exactly how it was on the big points:

'Joe Racket made the same mistake in the semis at Forest Hills in '38. He never recovered either.'

Needless to say, many of his observations will be suitably esoteric.

'Why on earth did he serve wide to Racket's forehand at 30 – all?'

'It's the same old story. He just can't seem to get his down-the-line topspin backhand working when he's returning serve against lefthanders.'

'Look at the way he's hitting back junk topspin with that high lazy bounce so that Racket has got to put most of the pace back in.'

'If Racket could take the ball earlier on his approach shots, and narrow the angles down more, he'd cut out those passing shots and force the sort of blocked returns that would be easy putaways.'

All comments will contain at least a smattering of jargon:

'He's staying with the ball better now.'

'It was after that third duster in a row that he began to choke.'

'He's just waiting for freshies. Then you'll try to see him hit the chalk.'

If you ask an experienced tennis talker the score he won't simply reply: 'Racket's losing'. He'll say:

'He's love – 40 down in the second against the serve having lost the first to four.'

There'll also be plenty of detailed technical analysis of the game. But the expert tennis watcher will also always come up with some devastatingly simple piece of advice, which, if the players were only told, would completely turn the game around:

'If Racket just stood in a foot more when he receives serve, every one of those returns would be a winner.'

'All he's got to do is hit steady roll topspin crosscourt to make Rocket volley up to him. He could then put it away every time.'

'He's a fraction late all the time. If he just took the ball a millisecond earlier it would be a different story.'

'All he need do is keep the ball in play. His opponent would beat himself.'

When watching your fellow Racketeurs rather than the professionals a somewhat different approach is called for. There's the same stress on technicalities, the same display of expertise, the same simple suggestions that could revolutionise the game, but it's all done with rather more tact and sympathy – particularly if these are people you might meet on court some day. Never imply that your fellow Racketeur might lack basic playing ability; suggest rather that it's some technical snag that's causing the problem.

'There's always so much wrist in Joe's shots. I don't know who taught him that semi-Western he seems to favour. I'm sure he'd do better with a full-Western.'

'The more I watch Joe play, the more convinced I am that he hasn't got that racket strung right for his game. He must have at least 65 lb there – too much for synthetic in a metal frame. He'd have a lot more control at 55. Either that or he should switch to gut.'

'I know most of the pros stay with a Continental for all volleys these days, but I'm not sure Joe wouldn't do better to adjust his grip. His racket face is just too closed on the backhand.'

Rules of Tennis

PAIRING UP

It's easier to get into a game than out of one.

Once you've played someone, you may have to play them again.

When someone says: 'We really must have a game sometime', he doesn't always mean it.

Anyone who invites you to play without having seen you play is probably not a very good player.

When you're invited to make up a four without being told who the others are, it pays to be suspicious.

Everyone avoids a novice.

Even a novice is welcome if there's no one else around and you need a fourth.

The best pairings are with the opposite sex – provided the girl lets the man win.

In any match at least one of the players will be wishing he was playing with someone else.

If you are commenting on a Racketeer you clearly regard as your inferior, you can afford to be somewhat more patronising:

'You'll never pick up a half-volley like that – you've got to learn to get down to those balls.'

'Why do you always have to play 'winner takes all' on the big points?'

'If you could just vary your backhand and go down the line instead of always that crosscourt slice.'

Frequently tennis-watchers will tend to wax philosophical, treating fellow spectators to a few generalities on certain aspects of the game.

'The high backhand volley is one of the most difficult shots in the game – so hard to hit it with power. The important thing is not to try to 'wrist' it and just let the forearm make the stroke. Still, he set it up well.'

'Lefthanders so often seem to have this problem of a vulnerable backhand. But there's a lot he could do to improve it.'

Usually, of course, these comments will be addressed to fellow spectators. There's no sense in annoying the players. To them you just say: 'Shot', 'Well played', 'Nice one, Joe'. But if the performers are manifestly inferior, you need not worry too much about sparing their feelings and can call out to them with your unwanted advice.

'Knees, Joe.'
'Don't run around your backhand.'
'Long steps.'
'Short steps.'
'Move.'
'Let it bounce.'
'Punch your volleys.'

Sometimes, if you manage to attract the player's attention, you can offer a little demonstration – all performed very discreetly of course, as if you don't want anyone but the player to see.

'See what I mean on the volleys – short and sharp, like a punch on the nose.' (The demonstration can be rounded off with a condescending wink.)

These players may not always thank you for your advice, but if you don't play them, it doesn't matter. If they're impertinent enough to ask who you think you are to give advice, it's best to disarmingly disclaim any expertise. You're just an innocent observer – but you would suggest they ask the coach what he thinks and perhaps take a few lessons.

Not only does a top-class talker convey that he's seen and played a lot of tennis, he's also played it *on every imaginable surface*. This experience, of course, he is always willing to share: He'll suggest that Joe's game would be much more suited to *grass*. Or that perhaps Joe should try playing on *wood* to sharpen himself up. Or that the outcome of the match would have been completely different if they'd been on the *soft dirt* courts of France with their low bounce, rather than on high-bouncing *Har-Tru*. Or that Joe's short approach shots which work so well for him on Uniturf would be suicide on grass or clay.

He's equally knowledgeable about rackets and balls. He may not wield a racket very well himself, but he's superb at twirling other people's in his hands, casting a critical eye over them and offering his professional opinion. A favourite gambit is to ask to see another player's racket as he comes off court. He'll then examine the instrument carefully as if to confirm suspicions and then inquire: 'Ever thought of changing your racket?' If the victim rises to the bait, our tennis watcher can then ramble on indefinitely about the merits and defects of different types of rackets and the more esoteric aspects of stringing – about why Borg strings his rackets at 80 lb plus while McEnroe prefers just over 50, the advantages of beef gut as against lamb gut, fine gut vis-à-vis thick gut, not to mention different types of stringing to suit particular conditions (looser string tension on a heavy day).

He'll also be full of interesting 'well I never' facts like: It takes seven sheep to supply the gut for one tennis racket.

He'll be equally well versed in the individual peculiarities of all the different types of balls on the market. These may all, in theory, meet the required standards (not vary from the norm by more than 1/16 inch in diameter, 1/32oz in weight, 4 per cent in rebound). But this permits enormous disparities in performance which our sideline expert will be only too happy to go into. Once again there will be plenty of opportunities for parallels with the past — explanations of how today's balls are harder to control (lighter and livelier) and how the wool-covered balls of the 30s were so much more responsive to touch.

Here, too, he'll be full of interesting facts like: 'A tennis ball loses half its kinetic energy in collision with your racket.'

Of course the great risk for the pro tennis watcher is that he gets branded as a know-all and a bore. But then most Racketeurs are — especially when they're on the sidelines. It's one of the game's golden rules that those watching always know more than those playing.

14. The Tournament

**'Seventeen successive double faults, probably a
record in a major championship, were served by Miss
M.H de Amorin (Bra) at the start of her first match at
Wimbledon in 1957'**

The Guiness Book of Tennis Facts and Feats

Whereas most Racketeurs handle the *big* tournaments rather well, they often fail to
live up to expectations (theirs) at the local club tournament. Many a carefully
constructed reputation and tender tennis ego are sorely damaged when the annual
ordeal comes around.

Defeat (the fact is that half of the entrants must lose in the first round) is not just a
short sharp shock – soon over and forgotten. The results (perhaps the ignominy of
being eliminated 1 and 2 in your opening match) will stay up on the club notice
board for months to come, curling up and yellowing at the edges, but still read and
re-read with interest – particularly on a rainy day. The problem is that you can't be
around all the time to explain how it *really* was in your match and how the scoreline
doesn't tell the *whole* story about what was actually *quite a close* game.

Nor will the knowledge of the facts of your defeat be restricted to a limited circle
of fellow Racketeurs. It's at tournament time that friends and relatives often decide
to stroll over to the club to pass the time of day and watch you in action. (You may
have made the mistake the day before of saying you were having an early night
before the Big Match). As your friends probably don't play tennis, but have been
led to believe (by you) that you do, they simply won't understand why your match
isn't a bit like Connors and McEnroe slugging it out. It'll be no good explaining that
most people don't actually play like Connors and McEnroe. However hard you
try, you'll never be able to convince your admirers that the hunchbacked senile
dwarf who thrashed you really is a very good player.

Would-be Racketeurs are therefore advised to stick with Wimbledon and Flushing Meadows and to give the club tournament a miss (both singles and doubles).
That goes for the Handicap Tournament as well. It's by far the simplest way of
avoiding humiliation by someone you don't know or had always regarded as your
inferior. And even if you were to get matched up with one of your regular playing
chums, you'd find it wouldn't be the usual cosy encounter you're used to.

So it's probably best to stay away from the club altogether during tournament
time. This is always a period when people are on edge and nerves are frayed.
Friends and lovers fall out when one of them chooses someone else as a doubles
partner. Friendships come to an end when people find they are drawn against one
another or when they team up for the doubles and get hopelessly beaten.

You'll find that people will change from one day to the next at tournament time.
All tennis players are competitive, especially so if they enter the tournament. But

suddenly everyone's pretending that they're not – pretending that they just entered *for the fun* of it. And don't believe any of that nonsense about 'loving your competitor because he brings out the best in you'. It doesn't apply to tournament tennis, where it surely brings out the worst.

Another good reason for staying away is that it's extremely difficult to get a court at this time, particularly in the early rounds, since tournament matches have priority. Actually, one of the few things to be said for entering is that at least you are guaranteed a court to play on – for as long as you manage to stay in the running that is.

You are also guaranteed to be upset by the way the seeding has been decided – although the club's low estimation of your talents may in the end work to your advantage. It's far better to be eliminated straightaway by one of the top seeds, even if it is 'love and love' (everyone will be in awe of you for just stepping onto court with The Monster) than it is to be knocked out by someone you would not normally deign to play. It's worth making an effort, however, to get through to the second round, since defeat in the first means you'll have to suffer further humiliation in The Plate Tournament for first round losers.

Despite it all, however, every year thousands of Racketeurs will be seduced, against their better judgement, by the lure of the glittering prizes. And, it must be admitted, getting to the club finals probably means as much to the average Racketeer as winning the Grand Slam. So for those who can't resist putting their name down or getting someone else to put it down for them (without their knowledge, of course) here's some advice:

Get your match over early. There's nothing worse than playing leapfrog with your opponent (each finding reasons *not* to play on the days proposed by the other), until you reach the deadline and the tournament referee forces you to play on a day that doesn't suit either of you. The only possible advantage in delaying the match is that it may enable you to get out of the whole thing by defaulting, or even earn you a walkover into the next round.

Preparation, of course is all-important. Try to ensure that the game is held on *your* terms – with *your* balls, at *your* time of day, in *your* weather conditions. If you're up against a strong opponent, try to get onto a lumpy back court (this provides you with an excuse and will enable you to take some points off him as a result of bad bounces). Against someone timid and shy, play on a front court when there are lots of people around. If you don't want witnesses, arrange to play away from the club altogether.

You should also be better armed with excuses than usual – first of all, for arriving late. It's always a good idea to keep your opponent hanging around a bit – though never quite long enough for him to be able to claim a walkover (unless, of course, you want to default).

When you do get there, don't hesitate to let your opponent know the handicaps under which you are playing. These can be physical injuries (you arrive with one limb heavily strapped). Or you've been playing nothing but doubles recently (unless, of course, it's a doubles match, in which case you've been playing nothing but singles). Or it's been all squash or badminton for you lately. Or you haven't been near the club for months (someone else evidently put your name down – it was a big surprise when your opponent rang). Or you've just spent a night on the tiles.

But no matter, you imply cheerily. After all, you were never one to make heavy weather of your woes. The hearty cheerful approach is important for responding to any excuses he tries to make. If he tries to tell you how *he's* just spent a night on the tiles, tell him about the time you turned up for the club semis a few years ago after not having been to bed that night and never played better in your life.

If, perchance, you have to wait to go on court, make sure you invite him to have a drink. This a) puts him in your debt, b) may dull his senses a bit (be sure to offer him alcohol) and c) shows up how seriously he's taking it if he refuses.

You, of course, are not taking it seriously at all. This will be shown by your somewhat sloppy turnout – unlike your opponent who has that freshly laundered look. For you this is just a game like any other.

Of course, this sort of bright and breezy approach can be a bit difficult if you're drawn against one of your regular partners. He'll know this isn't the real you. But even if you try to be your usual self, you won't succeed. Tournaments have ways of affecting your behaviour.

When you finally start playing you've just got to make the best use of all your standard ploys, applying them more thoroughly than ever. It is, for instance, more important than usual to give away nothing at all about your game in the knock-up.

The chances are that you won't play very well. This is the day you should be playing like a tiger, but in fact feel more like a lamb with a lead arm. Your game will probably be twice as erratic and uncontrolled as usual even though you are being twice as careful. It'll be the same for your opponent, of course. The deciding factor will be who is the least off his game. In tournaments, he who makes the fewest errors, wins.

Make sure you maintain your infuriating heartiness and chattiness throughout – particularly if you're winning. And if you do end up the victor, treat it all as a bit of a surprise: you didn't expect to do well, but the ball did seem to be rolling for you; it really was your day; perhaps it was the fact that your opponent was playing so well that brought out the best in you.

If, however, it didn't go quite the way you hoped and it's your opponent who has the privilege of leaping over the net and writing the score up, make sure you're well supplied with answers for replying to that dreaded question. 'How did you get on?' (People only ask you this when they know you lost. You never get asked when you win.)

The best sort of riposte is that you weren't taking the match seriously. You just went out there to have a game and paid the price. Silly, really. You should have put a bit more into it. You might also convey that there was something a bit *underhand* about his victory. You were a bit miffed by some of his calls. And you would have liked a bit more time to warm up – you hadn't played for such a while. He was obviously playing to win – steady percentage tennis – while you kept coming in, trying to make a match of it, trying to pick balls off your feet and throwing points down the drain as a result. Still, he did deserve to win. You hadn't really wanted to play, but someone put your name down and, in fact you rather enjoyed the game. You'd have enjoyed it more, of course, if it hadn't been for your injury (which didn't give you all that much trouble, not *really*). But if it hadn't been for the injury, and the fact that you had to play with your other racket as No. 1 racket was being restrung, it might have been a different story. You might also have done better if you'd been prepared to play on *that* day (it was a difficult week for you, but he insisted on playing then, so you agreed). But you won't make excuses. That's not your style. It was his game all right. Never complain, never explain, that's your motto. And when all's said and done, you're rather glad to be out, so that now you'll be able to concentrate on the league properly.

Some Racketeurs might have the honesty to put it another way. To quote that great tennis philosopher, Snoopy, once again:

'It doesn't matter if you win or lose – until you lose.'

Final Rules of Tennis

When you say 'thanks for the game', you aren't always very grateful.

The spectators who have been watching your match with the keenest interest are not mere spectators. They're next on court.

As you leave the court, there'll always be something left hanging on one netpost.

The way you tell it afterwards isn't always quite the way it really was.

At the start of every season you'll wonder if this might perhaps be *your* year.

By the end of the season, you will be wondering: 'Why ever do I bother?'

You will frequently reflect that tennis, like life, can be very unfair.

You'll pay your subs again next year.

They will have risen substantially since the previous year.
